W9-BJV-336

Reconstructing Italian Fashion

Dress, Body, Culture

Series Editor **Joanne B. Eicher,** *Regents' Professor, University of Minnesota*

Advisory Board:

Ruth Barnes, *Ashmolean Museum, University of Oxford*
Helen Callaway, *CCCRW, University of Oxford*
James Hall, *University of Illinois at Chicago*
Beatrice Medicine, *California State University, Northridge*
Ted Polhemus, *Curator, "Street Style" Exhibition, Victoria & Albert Museum*
Griselda Pollock, *University of Leeds*
Valerie Steele, *The Museum at the Fashion Institute of Technology*
Lou Taylor, *University of Brighton*
John Wright, *University of Minnesota*

Books in this provocative series seek to articulate the connections between culture and dress which is defined here in its broadest possible sense as any modification or supplement to the body. Interdisciplinary in approach, the series highlights the dialogue between identity and dress, cosmetics, coiffure, and body alterations as manifested in practices as varied as plastic surgery, tattooing, and ritual scarification. The series aims, in particular, to analyze the meaning of dress in relation to popular culture and gender issues and will include works grounded in anthropology, sociology, history, art history, literature, and folklore.

ISSN: 1360-466X

Previously published titles in the Series

Helen Bradley Foster, *"New Raiments of Self"*: African American Clothing in the Antebellum South
Claudine Griggs, *S/he: Changing Sex and Changing Clothes*
Michaele Thurgood Haynes, *Dressing Up Debutantes: Pageantry and Glitz in Texas*
Anne Brydon and Sandra Niesson, *Consuming Fashion: Adorning the Transnational Body*
Dani Cavallaro and Alexandra Warwick, *Fashioning the Frame: Boundaries, Dress and the Body*
Judith Perani and Norma H. Wolff, *Cloth, Dress and Art Patronage in Africa*
Linda B. Arthur, *Religion, Dress and the Body*
Paul Jobling, *Fashion Spreads: Word and Image in Fashion Photography*
Fadwa El-Guindi, *Veil: Modesty, Privacy and Resistance*
Thomas S. Abler, *Hinterland Warriors and Military Dress: European Empires and Exotic Uniforms*
Linda Welters, *Folk Dress in Europe and Anatolia: Beliefs about Protection and Fertility*
Kim K.P. Johnson and Sharron J. Lennon, *Appearance and Power*
Barbara Burman, *The Culture of Sewing*
Annette Lynch, *Dress, Gender and Cultural Change*
Antonia Young, *Women Who Become Men*

DRESS, BODY, CULTURE

Reconstructing Italian Fashion

America and the Development of the Italian Fashion Industry

Nicola White

Oxford • New York

First published in 2000 by
Berg
Editorial offices:
150 Cowley Road, Oxford, OX4 1JJ, UK
838 Broadway, Third Floor, New York, NY 10003-4812, USA

Berg is an imprint of Oxford International Publishers Ltd.

Library of Congress Cataloging-in-Publication Data
A catalogue record for this book is available from the Library of Congress.

British Library Cataloguing-in-Publication Data
A catalogue record for this book is available from the British Library.

ISBN   1 85973 336 0 (Cloth)
        1 85973 341 7 (Paper)

Typeset by JS Typesetting, Wellingborough, Northants.
Printed in the United Kingdom by Biddles Ltd, Guildford and King's Lynn.

For Matilda

Contents

Acknowledgements

I am especially indebted to Professor Lou Taylor for her practical and intellectual support, her profound understanding of the history of dress and for commenting on the text. I would also like to offer particular thanks to Dr Stephen Gundle, whose constant assistance and knowledge of Italian history proved invaluable.

I owe much to the many witnesses in Italy and the US who gave interviews and allowed me access to private archives: Micol Fontana, Couturier, Rome; Gianni Ghini, assistant to Giovan Battista Giorgini, founder of the Florentine fashion shows; Eleanor Lambert, PR, New York; Laura Lusuardi, founder-employee and Fashion Co-ordinator, MaxMara, Reggio Emilia; Achille Maramotti, Chairman of MaxMara, Reggio Emilia; Beppe Modenese, founder of the 'Milan Collezione'; Maria Pezzi, fashion illustrator, Milan; Luigi Settembrini, PR and writer, Florence; Carla Strini, assistant to Emilio Pucci, Florence; and Enzo Tayar, fashion buyer, Florence. I am enormously grateful to Milanese journalist Elisa Massai, not only for allowing me to interview her, but also for letting me see her extensive archive of *Women's Wear Daily* cuttings, which formed a key element of the research.

I would also like to thank those who gave important leads, either in interview or in correspondence: Giorgina Appignani, Polimoda, Florence; Bonizza Giordani Aragno, dress historian, Rome; Cristina Brigidini, Pitti Immagine, Milan; Gianni Brovia, Moda Industria, Milan; Dr Anna Bull, economic historian, University of Bath; Cally Bush, Italian-American Museum, San Francisco; Grazietta Butazzi, dress historian, Milan; Dr Patricia Cunningham, dress historian, Ohio State University; Professor David Ellwood, economic and political historian, John Hopkins University, Bologna; Mr Fignatelli, Italian Cultural Institute, San Francisco; Sybilla della Gherardesca, Pitti Immagine, Florence; Dr Paul Ginsborg, social and political historian, University of Florence; Giorgio Guidotti, PR, MaxMara, Reggio Emilia; John Harper, economic and political historian, John Hopkins University, Bologna; Larry Lachman, former Chairman of Bloomingdales, New York; Judith Mathey, Secretary of the Costume Society of America, Earleville; Dr Alexandra Palmer, dress historian, Toronto; Stephania Ricci, Curator of the Pucci Archive and the Ferragamo shoe museum, Florence; Fiammetta Roditi, Tremelloni Library,

Milan; Dr Valerie Steele, dress historian, FIT, New York; Jean Toschi Marazzani Visconti, PR, Milan; and Vera Zamagni, economic historian, John Hopkins University, Bologna.

I am also grateful to the curators who allowed me access to the dress archives of public museums: Gloria Bianchino, CSAC, Parma; Shirley Goodman, FIT, New York; Rosemary Harden, Museum of Costume, Bath; Amy de la Haye, Victoria and Albert Museum, London; Melissa Leventon, M. H. De Young Memorial Museum, San Francisco; Phyliss Magidson, Museum of the City of New York; Patricia Mears, Museum of Brooklyn, New York; Alison Patterson, Royal Museum of Scotland, Edinburgh; Cristina Piacenti and Caterina Chiarelli, Galleria del Costume, Pitti Palace, Florence; Emma Young and Rebecca Quinton, Brighton Museum and Art Gallery; and Susannah Worth, FIDM Museum and Library Foundation, Los Angeles.

Finally, I thank Luigi Maramotti, Vice-President of MaxMara, for providing the funding which made this research possible, Professor Ian Griffiths, School of Fashion, Kingston University, for introducing MaxMara and for arranging the funding, and my husband Christopher Mascall, for taking photographs, commenting on the text and unending patience.

List of Illustrations

Introduction

As the new millennium begins, the Italian fashion industry is unquestionably one of the top three players on the international fashion stage and ranks parallel with Paris and New York.[1] Yet before 1945, there was no industrial production of fashionable womenswear in Italy, and little innovative made-to-measure haute couture. The well-known Italian fashion style currently seen in the world's glossy fashion magazines rose seemingly from nowhere in the post-war years, and was not widely recognised until the early 1980s. It is perhaps not surprising therefore that the early post-war period has been seen simply as a preparation for the recent 'miracle' of Italian fashion. This book seeks to correct this impression by viewing these years as the unrecognised foundation of the post-1980 success. It considers whether a distinct Italian fashion look existed in the mind of the international fashion industry in the post-war period, by viewing Italian fashion as a product which represents a complex mixture of foreign inputs, domestic responses and original developments.

Until recently the study of fashion met with widespread disapproval, or at best neglect, within academia. To enjoy the study of dress was to risk being labelled intellectually shallow and vain. In the words of American dress historian Valerie Steele, 'fashion was widely regarded as frivolous, sexist, bourgeois, "material" (not intellectual), and therefore, beneath contempt'.[2] Today, happily, fashion is seen as far from trivial in academic circles. Scholars across many disciplines recognise it as a potent form of communication, which can tell us much about the cultural, economic and social history of the society in which it is worn. Thus the history of fashion has become a rich area of research and interpretation and has moved 'from the wings to center-stage'.[3]

The intricacies of this evolution have been explained at length by the various contributors to the December 1998 'Methodology' issue of *Fashion Theory* which highlighted two major trajectories in the field of fashion which have polarised its study in the last twenty years. Firstly, the often uncritical dress history tradition and secondly, the more recent theoretically centred exploration which has emanated from the development of cultural studies as an academic discipline. Traditional dress history texts have been dismissed as uncritical 'hemline histories', which focus on a chronological stylistic progression.[4] On the other hand, many dress historians have felt that their subject has been appropriated by theorists with little concern for historical context, and 'buried in complex and inaccessible language'.[5] It is now clear that it is possible to steer a path between traditional dress history and purely theoretical explanations in order to develop the benefits of both approaches, whilst simultaneously drawing on contexts from a range of related disciplines.

The use of a multi-disciplinary approach, rather than a prescriptive reading of history, has been the subject of considerable debate in the last decade, and is proposed, for example, by Christopher Breward in his recent book *The Culture of Fashion*.[6] Thus, this book examines the evolution of the Italian fashion industry from an interdisciplinary perspective. It uses economic, political and social history, as well as relevant debates, such as that surrounding style and national identity, to provide a more fluid framework for the study of fashion through empirical research, oral history, film and printed archival material. The logic of such an approach is especially appropriate for investigating the modern period, with its surviving witnesses, and varied media. The main problem of using an interdisciplinary methodology is knowing which research areas to draw upon, since the selection of disciplines can be overwhelming and endless. For this study, stress on the identification and analysis of objects led naturally on to other research areas, and analysis of the artefacts supported related documentary evidence.

In *Design History and the History of Design* (1989), John Walker set out just such a multi-disciplinary methodological approach. Walker suggests a way in which published and archival sources, together with oral history and audio-visual records, may be analysed. Walker stresses the significance of the relationship between production, consumption and the designed object, and the necessity to investigate both object and the context of research in other fields, such as economic history and theoretical work. However, few recent multi-disciplinary studies base ideas around analysis of objects, or 'material culture': images of objects are sometimes used to illustrate texts, but are rarely used to support findings. Yet it is this very issue that seems to be at the heart of the current debate surrounding dress history methodology. 'Material objects matter,' as Ann Smart Martin explains, 'because they are complex, symbolic bundles of social, cultural and individual meanings'.[7]

The significance of artefacts to the study of dress history was addressed firmly by Alexandra Palmer writing in *Fashion Theory*. Palmer proposed that: 'linking documentary data to material culture . . . enables scholars to contextualise artefacts and documents in a multi-layered fashion'.[8] Although the appropriate methodology for material culture analysis has aroused much recent debate, Palmer explains that: ' a material culture analysis . . . can be supplemented with the oral histories of those who designed, made, sold, bought or wore the garments. These histories can be amplified by archival research, both documentary and visual, as well as by contemporary newspaper and magazine reports, and theory from a number of fields.' Thus, a multidisciplinary perspective, based around material culture analysis, has been used in this research to examine the evolution of the Italian fashion industry.

The 'style' of the objects studied is also the subject of contemporary research, not least, as Stuart Ewen explains, because it is a 'basic form of information' and 'has a major impact on the way we understand society.'[9] Style is clearly a fundamental expression of culture and its significance to issues of national identity has been addressed recently by a number of authors, including Amy de la Haye, who writes that 'whether inadvertently absorbed or fully exploited by fashion designers, national identity offers a route to product determination and makes good business sense.'[10]

The evolution of an Italian national style in fashion has never been defined and neither has the specific character of its post-war development. Before the relatively recent rise of Italian fashion stars, from the mid-1970s onwards, most fashion histories did not even mention the presence of Italian Fashion, or made only passing mention to the most famous designers, such as Pucci.[11] Even the well-respected historical studies of Italian design have largely ignored the significance of Italian fashion, despite the fact that international interest in Italian fashion was so high in the post-war years.[12] In retrospect it is clear that Italian fashion of this period is much more culturally and economically important, both nationally and internationally, than has generally been thought. In the latter years of the twentieth century it has been the subject of a number of books by Italian authors, but many of these are inadequately researched and written and none explore the importance of the American market in any detail.[13] Even the 1991 Italian 'Ready-to-Wear' conference papers, failed to reveal any relevant information.[14] There is still no detailed historical or cultural analysis of the Italian fashion industry in the twenty years following the Second World War, though there is an increasing scholarly interest in Italian dress history. The work of Italian historians such as Bianchino, Butazzi and Aragno provides a valuable historical background. The only source which usefully explores the importance of America to Italian fashion in this period, is Valerie Steele's chapter, entitled 'the American perception of Italian Fashion 1943–68', which was published in the catalogue to the *Italian Metamorphosis 1943–1968* Exhibition, at the Guggenheim Museum in New York, in 1994, but this did not use Italian sources and the socioeconomic and cultural context of the US involvement in Italy's post-war reconstruction was not considered.[15]

Whilst therefore, there has been little published assessment of America's role in the development of the Italian fashion industry between 1945 and 1965, in the last few years, lively discourse in Italian, British and American

Universities has resulted in a variety of publications which analyse Italy's post-war political, socio-economic and cultural development, and in particular the role of the US within that. Two important examples of this type of study are, firstly, Paul Ginsborg's *A History of Contemporary Italy: Society and Politics 1943–1988* (1990), which is the first and most sound account of the relationship between society, politics and economics in post-war Italy. Secondly, Christopher Duggan and Christopher Wagstaff's *Italy in the Cold War: Politics, Culture and Society 1948–58* (1995) is the most recently published cultural-political analysis of the immediate post-war period . The papers in this book are taken from the conference 'The Politics of Power: Italy in the Cold War Period', at the University of Reading (October 1990). This was the first UK conference devoted to Italy in the Cold War years, and demonstrates the rich and varied current research on the period, by both English and Italian speaking academics. Recent interest tends to focus on two areas: the political and economic consequences for Italy of a new world order, and the impact of the US, especially American-style consumerism, on Italian culture. This book reflects these concerns and takes the context of both these areas of discourse and applies it to the development of the Italian fashion industry.

The three principal sources which offer evidence for an international commercial understanding of a distinct 'Italian look' in these post-war years, are: analysis of surviving garments in museum and private collections, oral history, and contemporary fashion press coverage. A number of relevant public garment holdings in Italy, the US, and the UK have been considered, notably the Pitti Palace collection in Florence, the archive of the Fontana couture house, Rome, and the M. H. De Young Memorial Museum collection, San Francisco.[16] Analysis of these clothes is set within the methodological framework provided by American dress historians Joan Severa and Merrill Horswill, who in 1989 published a useful method for the analysis of costume as material culture and explain that: 'the costume artefact, when subjected to formal analysis, may be expected to reveal evidence of attitudes, belief systems and assumptions which shed light upon a culture'.[17] Severa and Horswill's recommendations are applied in the assessment of garments for this thesis. They suggest: 1. Determination of the modal type of sample; 2. Analysis of artefacts for: material, design and construction, workmanship; 3. Examination of these in terms of: identification, evaluation, cultural analysis, interpretation and intuitive analysis. In cases where documentation of the garment is limited, this may be the only way to elicit information. Documentary evidence survives in the form of some fashion house archives, collections of media records, and some private archives. The most significant are the archive of Italian ready-to-wear manufacturer MaxMara, of Reggio

Emilia, and the records of journalist Elisa Massai and fashion illustrator Maria Pezzi.

Since most Italian fashion and textile houses have not kept archival records of the 1945–65 period, oral history has become a vital area of research for this study, both by necessity, and because results proved so informative. In *The Voice of the Past: Oral History* (1978), Paul Thompson described the ways in which oral sources can be collected and used. Thompson proposed that interviews with witnesses to past events can be an immediately rich and varied source of evidence for the historian, when placed in a wider context, and seen in terms of inaccuracies and bias. He points out that 'the memory process depends not only upon individual comprehension, but also upon interest'.[18] Many pioneering manufacturers of the immediate post-war period remain central players in the 1990s. A number of key witnesses are still alive, and interviews with manufacturers, designers, buyers, journalists, PR consultants, and assistants to the protagonists provide a rich source of hitherto unseen and unheard evidence.

In the light of this evidence, I propose that the United States of America played a vital role in the post-war evolution of Italian Fashion, in a number of closely related ways. Firstly, through initial financial support and close involvement in the industrial organisation of Italy; secondly, as a supplier of progressive manufacturing methods; thirdly as a cultural model, and fourthly, as a keen market. This role has never been explored in detail in relation to the fashion industry. The first chapter assesses the role of America in the Italian post-war reconstruction, before exploring the contribution made by the US to the regeneration of the Italian textiles industry, which was then well placed to assist the evolving Italian fashion industry. The second chapter considers the importance of US interest to the expansion of Italian fashion, especially the move into mass-production, in terms of production methods and markets. The third chapter focuses on the evolution of Italian style in fashion, and defines the formation of its key components. The final chapter analyses the relationship between this style and American cultural forms, pinpointing the way in which the Italian fashion industry responded to these stimuli, and ultimately, how Italian fashion was actively promoted in the US.

The dates chosen, 1945–1965, enclose an era of rapid economic, social and cultural change in Italy. The period of study begins in 1945, which marks the end of the Second World War and the start of Italy's post-war reconstruction, in which the US played such a significant part. The upper boundary is 1965 because by this time the Italian fashion industry had completed the primary development stage analysed and highlighted by this research, and had begun re-organisation entirely on its own terms, which led finally to the emergence of Italy as a major international stylistic and economic force in international fashion. This secondary development is beyond the scope and intent of this study. The research concentrates on the womenswear market because this is where the principal US market for Italian clothes lay. The enquiry is confined to the upper levels of Italian fashion manufacture, and which led the move towards international recognition, where more evidence survives.

Notes

1. This book uses Christopher Breward's definition of fashion as 'clothing designed primarily for its expressive and decorative qualities, related closely to the current short-term dictates of the market, rather than for work or ceremonial functions'. Breward, Christopher, *The Culture of Fashion*, Manchester University Press, Manchester, 1995, p. 5.

2. Steele, Valerie, 'Letter from the Editor', *Fashion Theory*, 1, March 1997, p. 1.

3. Styles, John, 'Dress History: Reflections on a Contested Terrain', *Fashion Theory*, 2, December 1998, p. 387.

4. For further details see Taylor, Lou, 'Doing the Laundry? A Reassessment of Object-based Dress History', *Fashion Theory*, 2, December 1998, pp. 337–58.

5. Jarvis, Anthea, 'Letter from the Editor', *Fashion Theory*, 2, December 1998, p. 300.

6. Breward, Christopher, *The Culture of Fashion*, Manchester University Press, Manchester, 1995.

7. Smart Martin, Ann, 'Makers, Buyers and Users – Consumerism as a Material Culture Framework', *Winterthur Portfolio*, Vol. 28, 2–4, Summer-Autumn, 1993, pp. 141–57. See also the introduction to Brewer, John and Porter, Roy, *Consumption and the World of Goods*, Routledge, London, 1993.

8. Palmer, Alexandra, 'New Directions: Fashion History Studies and Research in North America and England', *Fashion Theory*, 1/3, September 1997, pp. 297–312.

9. Ewen, Stuart, 'Marketing Dreams: the Political Elements of Style', in Tomlinson, Alan (ed.) *Consumption, Identity and Style: Marketing, Meanings and the Packaging of Pleasure*, Routledge, London, 1990, pp. 41–56. See also Ewen, Stuart, *All Consuming Images: the Politics of Style in Contemporary Culture*, Basic Books, New York, 1988.

10. De la Haye, Amy (ed.), *The Cutting Edge: 50 Years of British Fashion 1947-1997*, V&A, London, 1997, pp. 11–12. For further details of this debate see for example, Aynsley, Jeremy, *Nationalism and Internationalism: Design in the Twentieth Century*, Victoria and Albert Museum, London, 1993; Crowley, David, *National Style and Nation State: Design in Poland from the Vernacular Revival to the International Style*, Manchester University Press, Manchester, 1992; Hobsbaum, E.J.,

Nation and Nationalism since 1780: Programme, Myth, and Reality, Cambridge University Press, Cambridge, 1990 (second edition); Hutchinson, John, and Smith, Anthony (eds), *Nationalism*, Oxford University Press, Oxford, 1994.

11. See for example, Ewing, Elizabeth, *A History of Twentieth Century Fashion*, Batsford, London, 1974, pp. 171–2.

12. Even Penny Sparke's *Italian Design 1870 to the Present*, Thames and Hudson, London, 1988, devotes only three pages to Italian fashion.

13. The more reliable examples include: Butazzi, Grazietta, et al., *Italian Fashion, Volume 1: The Origins of High Fashion and Knitwear*, and *Italian Fashion, Volume 2: From Anti-Fashion to Stylism*, Electa, Milan, 1987.

14. Butazzi, Grazietta (ed.), *Per Una Storia della Moda Pronta*, Edifir, Florence, 1991.

15. Steele, Valerie, 'Italian Fashion and America', in Celant, Germano (ed.), *Italian Metamorphosis 1943-68*, Guggenheim, New York, 1994, pp. 496–505.

16. Other collections considered are: FIDM, Los Angeles; FIT, New York; Brooklyn Museum, New York; Victoria and Albert Museum, London; Museum of Costume, Bath; and Brighton Museum and Art Gallery.

17. Severa, Joan and Horswill, Merril, 'Costume as Material Culture', *Dress*, 15, 1989, p. 53.

18. Thompson, Paul, *The Voice of the Past: Oral History*, Oxford University Press, Oxford, 1988, (first published 1978), p. 103.

1

America and Italian Reconstruction

1. Italy at the end of the Second World War

When Allied troops first landed in 1943 Italy appeared to observers as a defeated nation, ravaged by the effects of war. Yet twenty years later it had been transformed out of all recognition to become one of the most powerful nations in Europe. This process has been described as 'The most profound social revolution in the whole of its history'.[1] The intentions and actions of the occupying forces proved to be a vital factor in the reconstruction and ensuing economic success of Italy.

Italy was at war for four years and a battleground for two. The industrial structure had been deeply marked by the experience of autarky and war under the Fascist regime. The consequent privations were arguably more severe than in any other Western nation. Between 1938 and 1945 a third of Italy's national wealth was destroyed.[2] Furthermore, nearly half a million people were killed and many more wounded. Destruction figures show especially heavy losses to housing, transportation, and industry and in 1945, industrial output was estimated at only a quarter of the pre-war levels.[3] Internal commerce had broken down through lack of transportation and goods to sell, whilst foreign commerce had been wrecked by autarky, wartime blockades and reliance on Germany, which was also in ruins. Foreign exchange and gold reserves had been used or stolen, so that Italy found it difficult to purchase the raw materials needed to reconstruct. Inflation was rampant and unemployment was so high that no-one tried to measure it. There was also the huge moral and political task of rebuilding out of the ashes of fascism; the goals of national superiority had gone and none had yet been established in their place.

In general, however, the prospects were not as catastrophic as this image suggests. Within little more than a year after the end of hostilities, a Constituent Assembly had drafted a new constitution for a republican form of government and the machinery of the new state was functioning in an orderly manner. Italy's economy was not entirely crippled and it was felt that wartime destruction could have been a lot worse. Although much industrial machinery was tired and antiquated, most of it had survived and for the most part, the damage to industrial plant was not as serious as was initially feared, especially when compared to that of other countries, Germany in particular.

Fortunately, the regions of greatest destruction did not contain any of the great commercial or industrial cities. In the North, the industrial centres suffered considerably from Allied bombardment, but not ground fighting and by liberating these cities before the arrival of the Allied armies, the Italian partisans succeeded in preserving the main factories from any further war damage. Textiles and clothing, located mainly in the North, were remarkably fortunate with only 0.5 per cent damage (of 1938 value) to a 16.1 million lire industry.[4] Factories were soon able to resume production, if they could obtain fuel and raw materials, and US aid was to prove invaluable in this respect. The international market was favourable, with consumer goods in short supply everywhere, and foreign buyers eager for Italian products. By the autumn of 1945, the Italian government was forecasting optimistic production levels for early 1946. Clothing was not included, but textiles had the highest projected output for any industry considered. As a percentage of pre-war output wool and cotton were expected to reach 180 per cent and artificial silk 50 per cent, against metal at 33 per cent.[5] The figures were over-optimistic in general, but the textile industry specifically met these expectations.

Allied Attitudes to Italy in the Immediate Post-war Period

The Anglo-American occupation of Italy began when troops first landed in Sicily in July 1943 and lasted until 1947. David Ellwood's *Italy 1943–1945* (1985) provides an authoritative analysis of the plans of the liberating forces in Italy, and in particular, the transfer of control from Britain to the US. Ellwood explains that control of the Mediterranean had been a strategic aim of the British for more than half a century. It was therefore Great Britain who exerted the main influence in Italy initially. Britain was also devastated by war, and Churchill was keen not only to protect his country's economy, but also to punish its former enemy. He maintained that Italy must 'earn its ticket back to the company of civilised nations', but did not feel that it was the task of the British to help them on their way.[6] A number of negative actions and opinions can be cited in support of this reading. They include a crippling devaluation of the Lire which made Italian economic recovery much harder and the action of the British Board of Trade in quashing early US plans to aid Italian industrial reconstruction, on the grounds that any revival of Italian textiles would threaten the Lancashire cotton industry.

The US clearly had different attitudes, and on major issues were consistently less hostile than the British. Europe, especially the British, tended to make their calculations in terms of past history, whilst the Americans looked to the future, to a world remade in line with the plans they were drawing up. These differences can perhaps best be summed up by the relative catch phrases for their Italian politics: the British intended to 'prevent epidemic and disorder' and the US to 'create stability and prosperity'.[7] This was the period when British influence in the Mediterranean decreased, US influence increased, and the uneasy collaboration between the 'great powers' came to an end. By the summer of 1945, a 'gulf of suspicion' separated the British and Americans from the Russians. The official start of the Cold War was marked by Churchill's famous Fulton speech of 1946, in which an 'Iron Curtain' around Europe was first mentioned. By this time the Americans had progressive plans for Italy. Furthermore, it was soon evident that the US was the only country to emerge richer from the Second World War than before it, and was in a position to bear the major financial burden for Italian relief and rehabilitation. Britain had little choice but to follow the American lead.

The reasons behind the US decision to take a fundamental diplomatic and financial interest in Europe were clearly a combination of politics, economics and ideology. Whilst historians have not yet agreed which was the greater motivation, it is accepted that the US felt it should intervene on a global level against Russia, initially at least, by economic means, in order to mould new conservative democracies based on material capitalism and unregulated markets. Harry Truman, President of the US after Roosevelt's death in April 1945, had long nurtured a desire to take an explicit stand against what he called 'Russia's remorseless desire for expansion'.[8] Italy, with its close proximity to communist Yugoslavia, was in a highly strategic geographic location, on what was to become the 'front line' in the developing Cold War. Italy also had a particularly strong Communist Party. As early as June 1945, the US Acting Secretary of State declared that 'our objective is to strengthen Italy economically and politically so that truly democratic elements of the country can withstand the forces which threaten to sweep them with a new totalitarianism.'[9]

Furthermore, three quarters of world capital and two thirds of industrial capacity was concentrated in the US at the end of the Second World War. Unless the US economy could find trading partners and sufficient outlets for its products it risked a return to depression and the possibility of diminishing political power in the face of the Russian threat. Europe represented an immense possible market, but had suffered greatly from the ravages of war and needed to be rebuilt. It was therefore seen as vital for the US to 'assist' in the reconstruction of Europe, and to create a favourable international capitalist trading structure, centred on exports. Exports were seen by the US as the only factor capable of breaking the vicious circle of the Italian economy, bringing badly needed markets and the capacity to import raw materials and technology. In the peace settlement of 10 February 1947, in which reparations payments were decided, Italy was treated with considerable economic leniency; Great Britain and the US asked for no reparations and worked very hard to keep the demands of other nations down.[10]

The Italian decision to pursue a close political and economic relationship with the US was made very early in the post-war years. The dominant American philosophy was that communism could only survive where poverty existed, and conversely, if poverty could be eradicated, so too would communism. The US 'Fordist' industrial model was based on the notion that mass-production, high wages for the poor and mass consumption, would eradicate poverty. By contrast, the pre-established European 'stratified' model included many different levels of production, which were aimed at existing markets, rather than the working classes.

As in the rest of Europe, there were many Italians who defended the European system in the inter-war period, as a protector of socio-economic distinction, and who attacked Fordism as a bourgeois version of communism. Nonetheless, there was a powerful enlightened elite (in both political and economic spheres), which was very attracted by the superior productivity of US technology and organisation, the resultant high levels of mass consumption, and the allied notion of Free Trade. This attitude was significantly reinforced by the receipt of US aid by the Christian Democrat Party during the Italian election campaign of 1948, and by the outbreak of the Cold War.

It has been argued that the concern to export was the prime motivator of all Italian government economic policy and that Italy faithfully followed US directives so closely that it was known as 'America's most faithful ally'.[11] The Italian Catholic Church support for this pro-US stance, for example, is illustrated in a speech given by Cardinal Spellman on 17 March 1948: ' I cannot believe that the Italian people will chose Stalinism against God, Soviet Russia against America – America who has done so much and stands ready and willing to do so much more, if Italy remains a free and unfettered nation.'[12]

The Marshall Plan

Soon after the defeat of the German Army in April 1945, Allied economic experts entered the industrial heartland of northern Italy. Their professed tasks were to restore production and employment (including the transportation and communication systems, to stabilise the internal monetary system), and to resolve traditional difficulties, such as the long-standing North-South disequilibrium. In 1946, when Italy had a trade and payment deficit of over

$500 million, the US directly provided $380 million through the United Nations Relief and Rehabilitation Administration (UNRRA), $98 million through the Foreign Economic Administration (FEA), and $110 million indirectly, through gift parcels and emigrant remittances.[13] In 1947, the US also gave Italy 'post-UNRRA aid' for the purchase of ships and foodstuffs. With little political dispute, 'reconstruction' was nearing completion and all was going according to plan, at least until mid-1947.

In 1946 and early 1947, Italian industry, especially the textile industry, experienced a 'mini-boom' which led to a belief that the recovery was further advanced than it was. In truth, raw materials were hard to obtain from abroad without the foreign exchange Italy needed to pay for it, and inflation (and the black market that accompanied it) was still out of control, making long-term industrial planning impossible. During the summer of 1947, a deflationary policy checked productive momentum, and a period of stagnation followed. Italy had been cut off from world trade for at least a decade, and was still a backward and poverty-stricken country, with few natural resources. Most industrial firms were tiny and Italy still had little ability to pay for imports, because stocks of foreign money were low, exchange rates were unfavourable, tourist trade was low, and international credit was poor. The US was a vital market for war-torn Europe, but America was not yet importing at pre-war levels.

Although America had helped Italy out of the initial crisis, assistance was given on an ad hoc basis, and did not form part of a long-term, rational plan of economic reconstruction. The Italian government decided to ask for this help in January 1947. Once the left-wing parties in the Italian government had been ousted, in line with American requirements, US Secretary of State, General George Marshall announced his country's plan for the reconstruction of Europe on 5 June. This was the European Recovery Programme, known popularly as the Marshall Plan.

Whilst no major study of Marshall Aid in Italy has yet been published, and the Marshall Plan records held in Washington, DC are incomplete with few details of 'on the ground' operations in Italy, the issue is addressed by both the broader socio-economic and political histories of Italy, and by intense research into the role of the Marshall Plan and the reconstruction of Europe.[14] Studies over the last few years conclude that the Marshall Plan played a crucial role in the Italian reconstruction and subsequent boom. Although the funds alone were not enough to stimulate economic growth, the Plan encouraged West European growth by 'altering the environment in which economic policy was made'.[15]

Despite the considerable scholarly attention to the Marshall Plan and Europe, the limits of documentary evidence mean that it remains much easier to study diplomacy and intentions of this period, rather than what actually happened in relation to Italian industry. It is still difficult to specify the workings of the Plan at the grass roots level, such as exactly who was responsible for distributing the funds, how much, to whom, and why. Nonetheless, it is possible to specify why funds were given, exactly how much Italy received and the Italian reaction. Under the Marshall Plan, the US promised aid, mostly in the form of goods, to Western European nations, for four years. The total contribution to Italy was more than $1,400 million.[16] The scale of Marshall Aid to Italy remains impressive: three ships per day and $1,000 per minute, according to a pamphlet for a Venice exhibition published in mid-1949.[17]

It is also possible to compare the use of Marshall Plan funds by the European nations. As an annual percentage of national income, net Marshall Aid represented 5.3 per cent in Italy, against 14 per cent in Austria, but only 2.9 per cent in West Germany, and 2.4 per cent in the United Kingdom, between July 1948 and June 1949.[18] This represented a significant income and at its height, the Plan represented approximately two years 'normal' growth to recipient countries. Italy received 11 per cent of Europe's total aid allocation; 80 per cent of this was in the form of goods, and the remainder in the form of loans on very favourable terms.[19] Significantly, Italy spent an increasingly high proportion of its aid on machine tools, rather than foodstuffs. As a percentage of all Marshall Aid financed shipments in 1952, for example, imports of machinery, vehicles, iron and steel products represented 20.6 in Italy, against 11.3 in Austria, 8.8 in the United Kingdom, and only 3.3 in Germany.[20]

The Plan specified that imports into each country, paid for by American aid should be sold and the proceeds in local currency should go into a 'counterpart fund', or *Fondo Lire*. Approximately two-thirds of the funds went to industry, railways and public works and did much to get Italian industry moving, and to awaken entrepreneurs to the possibilities of economic growth within their own economy. The degree of autonomy in the use of the counterpart fund is still debated. The money was spent on projects approved by the European Co-operation Administration, which was set up and run by the US, and distributed by the Italians. Although Paul Ginsborg (1990) suggests that US interest reached much further than Marshall Plan funds, and even within individual factories reached extraordinary levels in an effort to maintain settled economic expansion, it remains impossible to pinpoint how far the need for US approval controlled the payments to individual manufacturers at grass roots level.[21] However, it is possible to pinpoint US motives in the deployment of Marshall Aid.

Contrary to early accounts, the Marshall Plan was not simply a direct political result of the Cold War. The economic importance of the Plan is revealed in a statement regarding US intentions and the Marshall Plan, which was made by US President Truman, at the end of September 1948 to a small group of congressman at the White House: 'General Marshall has reviewed the trouble he is having with Russia in the United States, and Bob Lovett has given you the detailed picture. We'll either have to provide a programme of interim aid relief until the Marshall program gets going, or the governments of France and Italy will fall, Austria too, and for all practical purposes Europe will be Communist. The Marshall Plan goes out of the window and it's a question of how long we could stand up in such a situation. This is serious, I can't over-emphasise how serious'.[22]

The desired and crucial advantage for the US was the hastening of reconstruction, the weakening of the political left-wing and the transformation of debilitated European economies into the international capitalist system. It was the US intention that this transformation should involve increased production, the use of US raw materials and capital equipment, higher national standards of living, lower inflation, maximum employment, and increased exports. This in turn allowed an improved balance of payments, and a more competitive economy. American interests during the Marshall Plan years coincided to a high degree with how the Italian government defined its own interests. The very process of offering aid and asking Europeans to work out its application, tended to bring socialists, centrists and conservatives into coalition, because they shared a common economic view. At the same time this process excluded the communists, who were seen as a very serious political threat in the light of the developing Cold War. Thus it can be deduced that US political intervention in Italy was unnecessary once the Marshall Plan was underway, because the crucial political exclusion had already occurred.

However, recent literature stresses that Italy was not putty in US hands. For example, in *The Marshall Plan: America, Britain and the Reconstruction of Western Europe, 1947–1952* (1987), Hogan states that 'The American leaders needed their allies as much as their allies needed them. The Americans found it difficult to exert too much pressure on the Italian government, including pressure for more aggressive industrial development, lest this pressure strengthen the Communists, and tilt a precarious political balance in the wrong direction'.[23] The support and co-operation of those Italian politicians, businessmen and labour leaders who believed in economic growth, was absolutely essential to the US. Nonetheless, whilst some support was given strategically, other support had to be won. The most reluctant groups were amongst labour leaders, as well as some political and economic elites. This American dependence meant in practice that the Italians did have some leverage with the Americans and ultimately a great degree of control over their own destinies. It also meant that the US needed to promote the Marshall Plan within Italy.

In the re-assessment of the economic significance of the Marshall Plan, increasing attention has been given to its psychological impact. Indeed, David Ellwood describes the Plan as 'the most expressive form' of the 'powerful political and psychological impact of US influence' on Europe in the post-war period.[24] Ellwood qualifies this by saying that 'American power was turned into influence by their comprehensive and systematic insistence on the individual dimensions of the recovery-modernisation process'.[25] Clearly, the US sought to control not only the implementation of the Plan, but also its reception in Europe.

This was attempted through a remarkable propaganda campaign, which has been described as 'breathtaking in its size and ingenuity'.[26] James Dunn, the US Ambassador at Rome, made sure that this massive injection of funds did not go unnoticed by the Italian public. It is well documented that the arrival of every 100th ship of supplies was turned into special celebration; a different port of arrival was chosen and an overtly political speech given by Dunn, on every occasion. Often the goods were put on a special 'friendship train', then distributed ceremoniously at stations along the line. Whenever a new bridge or school was built with US help, Dunn spoke for America, for the 'Free World', and by implication, for the US-supported Italian Christian Democrat Party. Just in case the message was not clear enough, on 20 March 1948 Marshall warned that all help to Italy would cease if there was a Communist electoral victory. Furthermore, from within the US, the large and predominantly conservative Italo-American community organised a variety of initiatives in favour of the Christian Democrats; more than 1 million letters were sent to generally unrelated Italians during the election campaign, stressing the Communist peril, often containing a few coveted dollars.

The Marshall Plan was not solely responsible for European economic growth, but contributed significantly to it, by encouraging economic reorgan-isation and the opening-up of economies to foreign trade, especially with the US. Whilst reconstruction was largely complete by the time the Marshall Plan came on line, Italian industrial development was still backward and the payments crisis foreshadowed a serious collapse of critical dollar imports, together with a serious production crisis, which Italy could not have survived alone. The Marshall Plan offered the opportunity to make up for lost time and to purchase up-to-date technology from abroad, without all the risks and costs of research. It has been argued that Italian industrialists could hardly go wrong, even though some were in fact reluctant; technology was available, steel and energy costs were cheap, labour costs low, trade unions powerless, and money was sound. Furthermore, higher standards of living helped close the door to extremist political elements.

All they needed was a market, preferably protected at home and open abroad, and that is exactly what they got. In 1950 the Italian government introduced new import duties, much to the chagrin of the Americans. For a vital few years this defended domestic markets, which expanded as the Italian standard of living rose and export markets developed at an even greater rate; meanwhile consumption in Italy rose annually by almost 20 per cent in the fifteen years following the Second World War, industrial production almost doubled each year over the same period and the proportion of net income from abroad rose approximately six-fold in the 1950s.[27]

Historians now agree that the methods used by the Italians (or other Europeans) were not always ones approved by the US during the years of the Plan and that neither did Italian industrial production expand as far as its architects would have hoped. Moreover, the Plan did not alter the basic economic structure, nor did it help solve the fundamental problem of the North-South divide. Yet the Plan certainly helped Italy to overcome the devastation of the war period, probably saved her from economic deterioration and social unrest, and introduced an important new dynamic to the Italian economy. By July 1962 Italy had paid back all its Marshall Plan loans.

The Impact of the US Model of Manufacturing on Italian Industry

For nearly a century, the image of the US had been the most potent influence on the Italian people. Italians had emigrated there in their hundreds of thousands at the end of the nineteenth century; some had become very rich, and nearly all managed to send money home, contributing to the notion of America as a land of progress and plenty. However, it was not until the immediate post-war years that the Italian government aligned itself firmly with the US industrial and economic models. There is little doubt that at the end of the War, Italian industrial technology was unstandardised and unspecialised, the opposite of the American system of technology. There is also little doubt that the Americans made a concerted effort to apply their production model in Italy, and that it was the largest companies which were the first to take the opportunity to transform their plants with American machinery financed with Marshall Plan money.

In 1995, leading Italian economist Vera Zamagni examined the extent to which the American presence changed post-war Italian methods of industrial production and management.[28] Fiat, leader of Italy's motor car revolution, is the best-known example of this. Fiat, which had been a privileged beneficiary of Marshall Aid, made no secret of its admiration for US production methods.[29] As the markets for Italian industry grew, some smaller firms also began to update their equipment. For example, a 1957 survey of the Italian sewing-machine industry, led by Necchi of Pavia, stated that 'During the last two years, Necchi has been studying the latest American production scheduling methods with an idea to adopt the most suitable one.'[30]

It is clear that America led Europe in terms of management and industrial relations, as well as in technology and industrial organisation. Many 'study groups' of European entrepreneurs (including middle managers and foremen), including Italians, visited the US, often under American supervision, to learn about all these areas. Furthermore by this period, American management principles were taught both in US business schools and European universities, and could be studied through relevant published literature. Whilst it is still not known how far or how quickly these principles spread in Italian industry, Zamagni concludes that 'the American philosophy prevailed entirely, in industrial planning, marketing and machinery', although the Italians diverged in their preference for small plants, rather than large corporations.

The Italian 'Economic Miracle'

Despite US disappointment with the speed of economic developments in Europe, the late 1950s and early 1960s became years of unprecedented economic expansion in Italy, and of what has been termed the 'economic miracle'. The social effects of this have been analysed by Paul Ginsborg, in *A History of Contemporary Italy: Society and Politics 1943–88* (1990) who states that, despite the pervasive fundamental problems of the Italian economy, '1958–63 saw the beginning of a social revolution; in less than two decades Italy had ceased to be peasant country and became one of the major industrial nations in world'.[31]

Broadly, the 1950–70 period was a golden age for Italy's international commerce; trade in manufactured goods increased six-fold, economic integration of the major industrial countries reached new heights, and mass production for mass markets, both internal and external produced unknown levels of prosperity. Fordism and consumerism ruled. The lives of most ordinary Italians were transformed; family life, sexual attitudes and consumption habits, including what they chose to wear, changed dramatically. Per capita income grew more rapidly than in any other European country, encouraged by the unprecedented expansion of advertising. Italians, especially those in the centre and north of Italy, spent much of their new disposable income on consumer durables and by 1965, half the population could watch a family set. Between 1958 and 1963 growth rates reached unprecedented levels: investments in machinery and industrial plant increased, industrial production more than doubled, and above all, exports became the driving force behind expansion. The effect of the creation of the Common Market in 1958 is clear; Italian industry had reached a level of technological development and had a sufficiently diversified range of products to be able to react positively. The percentage of Italian goods exported to EEC countries almost doubled in the decade following 1955.[32]

It is significant to this study that the pattern of what Italy produced and exported altered considerably. Textiles and food products gave way to consumer goods which were in high demand in the advanced countries. This transformation was the result of a number of factors, including low cost and highly productive labour, the lack (until the late 1960s) of effective trade unions, the entrepreneurial skills of the owners of the new Italian firms and their ability to finance themselves in the early 1950s, as well as their willingness to adopt new techniques and introduce new machinery.

Conclusion

Marshall Aid, with its influx of American funds, machinery and know-how, played a deliberate and key role in opening up new horizons for many firms and in ending protectionism, which in turn revitalised Italy's productive system and was a strong impetus to modernisation. Higher productivity was met by higher mass consumption.[33] While the Italian government cannot be said to have planned the boom, it certainly contributed in many ways, such as the end of high inflation, non-tax of business interests, and favourable lending rates by the Bank of Italy, all of which served to create the correct conditions for accumulation of capital and its subsequent investment in Italy.

The creation of the Common Market, and the start of the Economic Miracle, in 1958, marks a watershed in this debate over the significance of the US to Italian industry. Before this date, it has been possible to determine the relationship and identify America's place in Italy's expansion. Once the economic boom amplified between 1958 and 1963, US investment, technology and markets lost their central position and took their place alongside the increasingly important domestic and European determinants.

2. The Textile Industry in the Post-War Period

The Economic Strength of the Italian Textiles Industry

Historically, textiles had been a strong export sector within the Italian economy, and had enjoyed a good reputation for centuries. Lombardy and Tuscany were leading centres of silk and wool production in the late Middle Ages, and silk manufacture was one of the key economic foundations of the cultural wealth of cities such as Venice, Florence and Lucca. In the nineteenth century, textiles played a vital pioneering role in the revolution of industrial production. The Milanese cotton industry is generally regarded as the first factory-based industry in Italy, and textile production is still more concentrated in the North than any other major branch of industry. In the early inter-war period, the industry as a whole enjoyed a growing international market, including the US. Large Italian firms were in the forefront of world rayon production. The silk industry, with its own breeding, spinning and weaving plants, had a particularly extensive US market. Although the majority of the textile firms remained small, by the outbreak of the Second World War there were a significant number of large internationally competitive companies in place and the industry was an important sector of the Italian economy.

However, it was not until after the Second World War that Italian fabrics acquired their international reputation. This is illustrated by couturier Micol Fontana's statement concerning Italian silk production, that 'Como was and still is the best in the world, but before 1951, no-body knew it.'[34] Relatively undamaged by war, most of Italy's textile producers were still operational in 1945, and were in a position to win much-needed dollars. Capacity was available, European, Asian and US markets were eager, and raw materials could be easily obtained from the Americans. The immediate post-war policy to export from Italy has been criticised by several economists, as a major cause of the subsequent speculation against the lira and inflationary pressures. However, in 1986, leading Italian economist Vera Zamagni underlined for the first time that the effort to revive Italian exports was particularly successful for engineering and textiles, both of which were to be industries key to the future development of fashion-related trade and industry.[35] Moreover, the principal textile competitors in Germany, France, Britain, and Japan were slow to revive from the War, and did not offer strong competition in these vital years.

The Deployment of US Aid to the Italian Textiles Industry

The Italian textiles industry was one of the most fortunate beneficiaries of the Marshall Aid programme in Italy. At the height of the Plan, Paul Hoffman, head of the Economic Co-operation Agency, produced a 'country study' of Italy. One of Hoffman's criticisms was that no overall plan of fund distribution had been evolved, and certain areas like steel and textiles were being 'indiscriminately favoured'.[36] Yet it seems unlikely that such powerful favours were granted entirely 'indiscriminately'.

The revival of the Italian textile industry was not simply in the interests of the Italians, it was a key part of US plans for Italy. US interest centred on the fact that it had huge stocks of raw cotton to clear, and that it wanted to promote private Italian exports, in order to move Italy towards a liberal commercial system. For this reason, the industry received assistance from the US State Department (and the American Embassy in Rome) in dismantling a series of bureaucratic and political obstacles, in order to secure US raw materials and the permission for key firms to use freely the foreign currency they acquired.

Direct aid to textiles was provided in two stages. Firstly, immediately after the War, vast shipments of old clothes were sent from America to clothe a stricken Italian population. Those that could not be worn were mashed and mixed with added fibres, such as nylon, to make it stronger, and then re-cycled as 'regenerated textiles' by Italian textile producers, especially those at the lower end of the market, based around Prato. Secondly, in October 1945, the Italian textile industry received a $25 million loan to pay for 150,000 bales of raw American cotton.[37] More than one witness has stated that these imports continued until 1949, and possibly into the 1950s; they consisted mainly of cotton, but there were also large quantities of wool.[38] This was a substantial sum and represented 25 per cent of the total European loan of $100 million for 600,000 bales.[39] Repayment of the loan required export of the finished products for dollars. They were also allowed to import the commodities they preferred, in the quantities they desired. It was the large and more powerful textile manufacturers, such as Rivetti and Marzotto, who benefited most from Marshall Aid, and as a consequence, they 'made a lot of money' in the late 1940s and early 1950s.[40] Clearly the interests of the Italian textiles industry exerted a considerable degree of leverage over economic policy, at least while their interests coincided with those of the US. There is no evidence that this relationship did not continue throughout the Marshall Plan years.

The Commercial Relationship between the Italian Textiles Industry and the US

The contents of the important Massai newspaper archive show that a proportion of Italian textiles was being designed specifically for the US market by 1949. Journalist Elisa Massai has a near complete private collection of her writings, which offer a unique insight into the trade links between the US and Italian fashion and textiles, published for the US market, yet written by an Italian, in Italy, over the 1949–63 period.[41] Massai wrote for Fairchild Publications which included *Women's Wear Daily* (*WWD*), the most important fashion trade paper in the US. Such detailed coverage indicates that Fairchild Publications played a major part in the communication of ideas and information between the fashion-textile industries of the two countries. One 1949 report reveals that 'styles being prepared for the American market include(d) white or gray silk crepes. Italian makers comment that they usually make separate collections for the US, but that European and South American buyers order from the collection prepared for the Italian market. This is largely a matter of colour preferences.' It is not clear exactly what proportion of textiles was created in this way, but evidently such fabrics were already seen to be a valued product in the US.

Direct communication between the Italian and American textile industries was enhanced through marketing trips to the US, by leaders of major Italian textile firms. In the immediate post-war years, marketing trips to the US by representatives of the larger textile firms of Como and Prato, desperately in need of markets, are commonly remembered. As Massai states: 'Italian textile reps were always travelling around looking for markets.' Achille Maramotti, Chairman and Founder of the Italian ready-to-wear company MaxMara, asserts that most of the Como silk producers, as well as big names in the wool trade such as Marzotto, frequently took selling trips to the US in the 1950s.[42]

Supportive evidence for this can be found in *WWD*. In November 1952, for example, a report stated that 'A sample collection of hand-woven Italian fabrics from Tessitura di Rovezzano, has been taken to the US.' By then, most of the larger companies also engaged US Agency Representatives, whose appointment was announced in the press, including, for example, that of the Royal Woollen Company for Laniera Tiziano of Milan, in 1952. In addition, *WWD* indicates that some major firms set up their own branches in the US in this period, including Terragni, who in 1949 were 'opening an office in New York, which will handle Canadian business as well as American'.

By the early 1950s, Italian textiles were also being promoted to the US market at 'Italian Handicraft' Exhibitions both in the US and Italy. For example, the Fairchild publication *Daily News Record* reported that Como fabrics had been selected for a 1950 travelling exhibition at the Brooklyn Museum. There were also International Textile Fairs in Italy (established in the interwar period), which were attended by American buyers. At the Milan Fair in April 1952, for example, the Italian-American Marketing Council was showing interest in Italian textiles, according to *WWD*. Evidently, by this time, the US market was as keen to import Italian textiles as the Italian textile industry was to export their wares. However, the relationship between the US and Italian textile manufacturers was not restricted to end products.

The Technological Relationship between Italy and the US

Until spring 1945, Italy's ally Germany was 'the God, in terms of technology' for textile manufacturers, according to Elisa Massai.[43] In the immediate post-war period, German technology was not available, and most new machinery came from Switzerland, which was nearby and neutral. However, by the late 1940s, machinery was available from a wider range of sources. It is Massai's belief that 'Italian manufacturers could not fail to be aware of American textile machinery and technology' because of their marketing connections, and the significance of Marshall Plan machinery to Italian textiles. The US cotton industry was technologically advanced, and cotton machinery became the most important technological import from the US to Italy from the early Marshall Plan years. No evidence has yet been found to show that other textile machinery was being imported from the US in these years, but at least one US manufacturer set up a production plant in Italy, as the Fairchild paper *Daily News Record (DNR)* reported in April 1960: 'A plant for the production of spindles and textile machine parts in Southern Italy is planned by Roberts Co. of Sanford, SC.'

The expansion of Italian-made textile machine production is more widely documented. It began in the 1950s, when Italians started working on improvements to their imported machines, and experimented with new technology. As early as April 1952, *WWD* reported that at the Milan Fair 'the interests of US visitors are centred mainly on textiles, accessories, textile equipment'. By this stage, Italy was selling its old textile machinery to developing countries and ex-employees and installing the most advanced technology in their plants, now often made by the increasingly sophisticated, innovative, and internationally competitive Italian engineering industry.

Although there is little information available concerning the use of Italian techniques and technology in the US, there are indications that the US imported a few innovative Italian textile techniques, such as the 'trichrome printing' process (from colour photography), which went into commercial textile production in Italy in the early 1950s. By the early 1960s, more and more equipment was being exported from Italy. For example, Italian synthetic leader Snia Viscosa was exporting machinery for nylon production to the Allied Chemical Company, and Snia technicians were sent to the US to start the plant. The value of the plant was estimated at a massive $45 million, plus royalties.[44] By this time Italian textile machinery was clearly internationally competitive, and the role of American machinery and techniques in Italian textile production had become negligible.

Rising Textile Exports

Italian textile manufacturers started exporting their fabrics to the US as early as the Reconstruction period and textile exports in general rose throughout the 1950s and early 1960s. The luxury silk market in the US became one of the largest for Italian goods. For example, in the first six months of 1952, total exports of Italian goods to the US were almost 50 per cent higher than for the whole of 1951.[45] It is highly significant that by 1960, Italy had overtaken its long-standing French rival Lyons, in this sphere. By 1954, the total export market of Italian apparel textiles (mainly luxury silks) was worth over $4 million and by 1960, almost $35 million.[46]

DNR indicates that these exports were not simply fortuitous, but were enhanced by government encouragement, via official textile governing bodies, such as the Italian Wool Manufacturers Association. Under the title 'Increased Sales to US urged on Italy wool mills', the paper stated in January 1952 that 'Italy could export 20 per cent of its wool production to the US without affecting the American wool industry because this represents only about 3 per cent of wool consumption in the US.' Renato Lombardi, President of the Italian Wool Manufacturers Association, said that the European and British Commonwealth countries had an excess output of wool manufactures which could not be absorbed locally. The solution, he believed, lay in promoting exports to dollar area countries: 'the moment is ripe for Italian wool manufacturers to get into the American market because of the growing interest in Italian styles and fabrics'. How far these governing bodies were manipulated by the Italian government and in turn by US intentions, is still unclear, for the reasons previously established.

Thus in the 1945–65 period, Italian textile manufacturers firmly established their products on the US market. Textile export was not just a one-way traffic, but available evidence indicates that it was not until the early 1960s that the US textiles industry began to market itself strongly in Italy, following the formation of the Common Market in 1958, seen now as a single entity. A November 1961 report in *WWD* illustrates this, saying 'following a lead established last season by Burlington Mills, the first US exhibitor to appear, five American manufacturers will appear on the roster of the tenth season MITAM international textile showmart opening November 29 in Milan, indicating growing interest in the Common Market'.

The Italian textile industry suffered a productive and competitive crisis in the 1960s, caused by both internal and external factors, including rising labour costs, inefficient distribution, obsolete plant, competition from new cheap-labour countries in the Far East, and sharp rises in raw material costs. This was followed, however, by extensive restructuring, with high levels of investment, great technological flexibility, and renewed international success.[47] Thus the industry enjoyed a period of specialisation and prosperity in the post-war years, and from this position was able to play a crucial role in the expansion of the Italian fashion industry.

The Relationship between the Italian Fashion and Textile Industries

The relationship between domestic textile and clothing industries is typically close in any nation. In France, the traditional leader of elite Western fashion, this relationship has been interdependent for centuries. It is possible to illustrate this with any number of historical examples, from Louis XIV's highly successful politically-motivated patronage of the luxury French silk industry, in the late seventeeth century, to the famous partnership between cotton millionaire Marcel Boussac and haute couturier Christian Dior in the post-war years. There is evidence that this same relationship existed in Italy after the War and that its development was to have a profound impact on the Italian fashion industry.

Massai remembers that straight after the War, vast reserves of materials originally destined for uniforms during the War and not used, were available to Italian dressmakers, because Italian textile plants escaped heavy bombing. This early post-war contact strengthened and extended the ties between the two spheres, as well as succouring the nascent Italian fashion industry. This mutually advantageous relationship developed rapidly from the early 1950s.

Financial and Promotional Links There are no examples of the full financial backing of Italian fashion houses by major textiles manufacturers, in the manner of Dior and Boussac, either at couture or ready-to-wear level, in these years. Nevertheless, all evidence indicates that aside from private individuals, textile manufacturers were the first to assist in the finance and promotion of Italian fashion after the War, in a number of specific ways. These ties can be dated from the early 1950s and had a dramatic impact on the growth of the Italian fashion industry. *Women's Wear Daily* offers firm evidence that textile manufacturers and dress designers were making promotional connections as early as September 1950. Under the title 'Italian Dressmakers and Wool Firms in Joint Showing', a report states that 'Biki and Noberasko of Milan, Fontana of Rome, and furrier Rivella of Turin' showed 'woollens supplied by Marzotto and Rossi of Valdagno, and Schio of Vicenza, Mabu of Milan, Zignone of Quarona, Fila and a number of Biella firms'.

Formal links between the Italian fashion and textiles industries began in 1952, and are described by Gianni Ghini, who helped Giovan Battista Giorgini to organise the first collective Italian fashion presentations.[48] Ghini stresses that 'a lot of leading Italian textile names were involved in the Florence fashion shows, almost from the start, in 1952'. This followed the meeting of a 'private committee' of the shows, in 1951 (the year the shows began), when committee member Count Stefano Rivetti, a leading textile producer, suggested that they contact other Italian textile manufacturers to obtain their sponsorship in return for the publicity associated with Italian fashion. Ghini was sent to the North as the envoy for the operation. His job was to arrange that a wide range of textile manufacturers paid L50,000 to each couturier for each model they produced using their fabrics. They were also asked to pay 'a certain amount' to Giorgini for the kudos of association and 'some exclusive publicity'. 'Sponsorship', according to Ghini, was not a word used in Italian fashion and textiles at this time, but that is indeed what this arrangement amounted to.

Count Rivetti, a famous society personality and influential manufacturer, knew most of the other manufacturers well, and his connections facilitated the operation. Some of the fashion designers also knew manufacturers, especially the Como silk producers, because they had already been using their fabrics for cocktail and evening dresses. At this time, Ghini recalls arranging formal sponsorship between Lane Rivetti (wool) and Veneziani, Linea Lane (wool) and Vanna, Val di Susa (cotton) and Vanna, Bemberg (cotton) and Veneziani, Ital Viscosa (part of Snia Viscosa, viscose) and Marucelli, Costa (silks) and Carosa, Tondani and Marucelli, as well as unspecified ties with Legler (velvets), Radiatrice (nylon), and a big group of silk manufacturers, including Terragni, Bedetti, Cognasca (President of the silk manufacturers association, who attended all the shows personally), Bernasconi and Ambrosini.

All these fashion designers were key figures in the evolution of the Italian fashion industry in the post-war years, and all showed at the new Florentine collections. Not all the manufacturers participated in the sponsorship in January 1953, but once three or four had agreed, they all rushed to join in, to the point in the late 1950s, where they wanted their own fashion-textile shows. These tie-ins were not simply promoted through the publicity surrounding the fashion shows. They were also presented in both editorial and advertising form in the fashion and textile press. Importantly, according to Massai, the textile companies even paid for the advertising.

Systematic analysis of *Linea Italiana* provides important specific evidence of this promotion. *Linea Italiana* was a post-war, seasonal, Italian fashion and textiles magazine aimed at a middle-high market level, as well as a mixed trade/public audience. It is subtitled 'I Tessili Nuovi' (new textiles) and this implied stress on textiles is reflected in the contents. There are more references to textiles than fashion in the early editions of *Linea Italiana*, and there are plenty of advertisements placed by textile and yarn manufacturers which feature tie-ins with high fashion designers. The earliest example traced is in the winter 1949 issue, and features dress designs by couturiers Curiel and Galitzine, including illustrations of the fabric used. The links between fashion and textiles continue to be promoted in later issues and the textile manufacturer is consistently named alongside the high fashion designer.

In the spring 1955 edition there is evidence of an important campaign formally linking Italian textiles with Italian high fashion, which is demonstrated in five pages of advertisements. Examples include the use of Costa fabrics by Carosa, synthetics by Snia used by Marucelli, and Faudella by Antonelli. In the same edition there is further evidence of the formal links between Italian textile manufacturers and Italian fashion designers. Seemingly an integral part of the report on the Florence fashion show, virtually every name is linked editorially to a sponsoring textile house. Typically, a half page shot of a designer model is supported by an editorial-style description, including full details of the textile used, and the names of both fashion designer and textile house printed in bold type. One example is shown in figure 1, a check waisted dress, photographed with a donkey, on location in an Italian village. The text reads ' "Jolly" is a new Marzotto fabric launched to coincide with the Florence shows of Italian fashion . . . it's beautiful, fantastic, modern and young'. The advertisement adds that 'Pucci has made the most of it in the particularly practical, fresh, and elegant model'. Clearly all these factors were important selling points for Marzotto.

By 1960, *Linea Italiana* was publishing extended publicity link-ups between fashion and textiles over many pages, through features such as 'Textiles for High Fashion'. Now the photographs of the couture models have reduced in relative size, to make way for reproduction of swatches of the relevant textiles. The captions still give a description of the model, but the names of the textile houses are printed in bold type and are given precedence on the page, indicating the purpose of the piece.

The Italian high fashion magazine *Bellezza* was established in 1941, as the official voice of Italian high fashion, and reveals further examples of the growing strength of formal links between Italian textile manufacturers and fashion designers. The July 1953 issue includes the first reference to such arrangements. A full page photograph is accompanied by copy which describes 'a Fontana model' (dress and evening coat) called 'Carnevale' in 'two tones of satin by Clerici Tessuto of Como'.

By February 1954, the silk manufacturers had formalised their links with high fashion even further. A *Bellezza* advertisement describes the thoughts of the Gruppo Fabbricanti Italiani Tessuti Serici Alta Moda (GFITSAM), the 'Italian high fashion silk manufacturers group', under the heading 'The fabrics which will be worn'. Evidently, the predictions of the Italian silk manufacturers were considered valuable by the high fashion press and its readership. Two months later, the same group presented 'a list of textiles which will become the models of spring-summer 1954' and beneath it, 'a list of the Italian fashion houses which will be using them: Marucelli, Vanna and Veneziani of Milan, Guidi of Florence, and Antonelli and Carosa of

Figure 1. Pucci check dress made in 'Jolly' fabric by Marzotto. This fabric was launched to coincide with the Florentine shows of Italian fashion. Source: *Linea Italiana*, Spring 1955, p. 28.

Rome'. This confirms Ghini's claim that following the initial arrangements in 1953, many others joined in.

However, the marriage between the Italian fashion and textiles industries was not always a happy one. Ghini states that at first, the fashion designers were often not happy with the quality or design of the cotton and wool textiles (though silk was not seen to be problematic, because the industry had a long history of making for haute couture, especially French). This is described as a difficult situation, but quality improved swiftly from that point, and was soon of an acceptable standard. From these official measures, as we have seen, promotional ties also developed in a less formal way, and the textile houses were often mentioned in press reports alongside the designer using their products, when no 'official' link had been made. One example of this is a *WWD* story from January 1955, which reports that Emilio (Pucci) 'showed a special group designed in wool from Marzotto, gossamer thin, but not transparent'.

The textile manufacturers were very keen to use Italian fashion designers to promote their materials, because it was extremely cost-effective publicity, and enhanced the elite status of their fabrics, as well as promoting their national interests. The couture houses did not generally have the money for extensive promotion and advertising, but the textile houses did and they undoubtedly helped to promote Italian high fashion in the process. Italian ready-to-wear manufacturers were not yet seen as cost-effective publicity, because they were not yet newsworthy, nor of high enough fashion status.

Flexibility and Innovation   There is also evidence that textile manufacturers created 'exclusive' fabrics for both individual ready-to-wear manufacturers and couture designers, as in France, rather than simply creating ranges from which all fashion producers could select. Gianni Ghini is clear that textile manufacturers 'did do exclusive fabrics', and this statement is confirmed by the testimonies of three key manufacturers working at different levels in Italian fashion. Micol Fontana, Rome couturier since 1943, remembers using, for example, Botto for wool, and Ambrosini and Clerica Tessuto for silk. Fontana recalls a 'very special relationship' and described how they would 'work together to create fabrics. Sometimes these would be entirely exclusive.' She concluded that 'textiles were vital to our success'.

Carla Strini, Head of Foreign Operations at the 'boutique' (designer ready-to-wear) label Pucci (1954–8), states that Pucci's silks were 'all printed in Como by Ravarsi, to Pucci's designs'.[49] Wools were made in Biella and cottons often came from a firm near Bergamo. Pucci's original idea would be passed to a husband and wife team who bore the title of 'designer', but who were not strictly creative. They translated the idea, and this was then taken to the textile printing factory for short-run, exclusive production. Such arrangements, Strini explains, 'were inseparable from Pucci's success'.

Achille Maramotti of MaxMara, dates the 'special rapport' between Italian fabric and clothing manufacturers as early as 1952–3. This, Maramotti says, is when the fabric manufacturers were finding it increasingly difficult to sell to their traditional retail outlets, because more and more of these shops were moving over to the sale of ready-to-wear. Therefore, they needed to develop a mutually beneficial relationship. Initially, the problem for MaxMara was that the existing fabrics were not suited for industrial production. Delicate materials which required careful hand-pressing were not ideal for the new industrial steam-presses, so the textiles industry had to produce a new stabilised cloth which would not shrink in the steam. According to Maramotti, the textiles industry was increasingly prepared to design according to the requirements of the ready-to-wear industry; exclusive fabrics were therefore available almost right from the start.

Moreover, once the textile manufacturers realised that MaxMara was a trustworthy and valuable client, they gave the company long payment terms. All interviewees, at both top ready-to-wear and couture level recall the availability and significance of such arrangements. Elisa Massai states that terms of six to nine months, and sometimes up to a year could normally be negotiated. Maramotti is sure that without these concessions, his company 'would not have been able to grow at such a rate, since the banks would not take such an untested risk'.

A combination of these factors meant that Italian couturiers and ready-to-wear manufacturers used Italian fabrics almost exclusively. Nearly all textiles were available, including silks, wools, cottons and most synthetics, although linen and some synthetics were not yet the forte of the Italian manufacturers. In the 1950s, MaxMara worked with woollen textiles from Loro Piano, Rivetti, Faudella, Trabaldo, Marzotto, and Ferrarin, silk from Camisci, Terragni, Ones and Mantero, of Como, cotton from Solbiati, and linen from French manufacturer Agache.[50] The international reputation of the Italian textiles industry grew throughout the post-war period, and became associated particularly with high-quality, innovative fabrics and designs. The silk industry in particular moved towards the manufacture of new, imaginative cloths for a luxury market. Indeed, Massai is adamant that they were 'stylistically, always a year or two in advance of international fashion'.

The Significance of US Aid to the Development of an Italian Fashion Industry

In view of the post-war Italian industrial experience outlined in the first section of this chapter, it is significant that there is no evidence that American-run Aid programmes directly assisted Italian fashion producers at any level. This is probably because the aid tended to go to large-scale manufacturers, and there were none in Italian fashion in this period. Gianni Ghini is certain that at high fashion level 'not one cent was paid by the government for promotion, press or publicity' during the Marshall Plan years. However, Massai recalls some limited 'organisational and promotional support', such as that given through the Salone Mercato Internazionale dell'Abbigliamento (SAMIA). SAMIA was an exhibition and market for the ready-to-wear industry, which was set up in 1954 to replace the 'Ente Nazionale della Moda Italiana'.[51] Massai also remembers several 'missions' to promote Italian fashion in the US, (as well as one or two, in the 1960s, to Russia and Japan) which involved some government funding.

For example, in 1958 the Italian Minister of Foreign Commerce, Guido Carli, organised a government-financed Italian high fashion tour of the United States. Carli asked Massai to accompany the tour, because he felt that she understood the US market. The tour showed both haute couture designs and the slightly cheaper boutique collections in each major US city; they began in New York, then went on to Washington, Chicago, San Francisco, Los Angeles, Dallas and Boston. These cities were selected because they were home to the major department stores which were such a crucial market for the Italians. The tour lasted about two weeks, and was solely for promotional purposes; nothing could be sold because the collections had already been shown in Florence and orders had been placed. It received considerable publicity, with both television and press coverage. Money was collected at the shows and it was given to an American charity, which can only have been good publicity in itself. Needless to say, as a public relations exercise, the tour was highly successful.

Conclusion

It is evident that US aid programmes assisted the Italian fashion industry, indirectly, rather than directly. The first section of this chapter established that US assistance played a part in the post-war regeneration of the Italian economy and helped to improve the standard of living, which created favourable conditions for the evolution and expansion of the Italian fashion industry. The latter section of this chapter has shown that the Italian textiles industry played a key role in this transition. Its significance, for the developing fashion industry, in terms of promotion, flexibility, and innovation is encapsulated in Massai's comment that 'Italian textiles were the most important factor, about 60 per cent, in the success of the Italian fashion industry.' In turn, the US played a key role in the success of the rapidly emerging Italian textiles industry, by ensuring its regeneration in the immediate post-war period, through its aid programmes, through its markets, and to a lesser extent (and for a shorter time) through its technology.

Notes

1. Ginsborg, Paul, *A History of Contemporary Italy: Society and Politics 1943–88*, Penguin, London, 1990, p. 1.

2. Clough, Shephard B., *The Economic History of Modern Italy*, Columbia University Press, 1964, p. 286, quoting 'Annuario della Congiuntura Economica Italiana, 1938–47', Vallechi, Florence, 1949, p. 1.

3. Ibid., p. 288.

4. Woolf, S.J. (ed.), *The Rebirth of Italy 1943–50*, Longman, London, 1972, p. 158. By contrast the 'metal' industry suffered an estimated 25 per cent damage.

5. Ibid., p. 159. Statistics compiled under the direction of the Banca d'Italia, in autumn 1945.

6. Ginsborg, Paul, *A History of Contemporary Italy: Society and Politics 1943–88*, Penguin, London, 1990, p. 40.

7. These phrases are quoted by Ginsborg, ibid., p. 41.

8. Ibid., p. 78.

9. Ibid., p. 79.

10. According to Clough, Shephard B., in *The Economic History of Modern Italy*, Columbia University Press, 1964, p. 286, Italy was required to pay $100 million to the USSR, $125 million to Yugoslavia, $105 million to Greece, $25 million to Ethiopia, and $5 million to Albania, over seven years. Clough's data is selected from the National Annual Statistical Abstracts.

11. Ginsborg, Paul, *A History of Contemporary Italy: Society and Politics 1943–88*, Penguin, London, 1990, p. 158.

12. Ibid., p. 116.

13. Clough, Shephard B., *The Economic History of Modern Italy*, Columbia University Press, 1964, p. 299.

14. See for example: Ellwood, David W., *Rebuilding Western Europe: America and Postwar Reconstruction*, Longman, London, 1992.

15. Dulles, Allen W., introduction to Bradford De Long, J. and Eichengreen, Barry, *The Marshall Plan: History's Most Successful Structural Adjustment Plan*, Discussion Paper Series 634, Centre for Economic Policy Research, May 1992. This point refers specifically to the conditions imposed for the receipt of US aid.

16. Ginsborg, Paul, *A History of Contemporary Italy: Society and Politics 1943–88*, Penguin, London, 1990, p. 158. According to the US International Co-operation Administration, 'US Foreign Assistance', Washington D.C., 1961, p. 15, quoted in *The Economic History of Modern Italy*, Columbia University Press, 1964, p. 30, these and subsequent arrangements resulted in Italy's receipt of $3,447 million in total economic aid between 1946–61.

17. Ellwood, David W., 'Italy, Europe and the Cold War: Politics and Economics' in Duggan, Christopher and Wagstaff, Christopher (eds), *Italy in the Cold War: Politics, Culture and Society 1948–58*, Berg, Oxford, 1995, p. 34.

18. Milward, Alan S., *The Reconstruction of Western Europe 1945–51*, Methuen, London, 1984, p. 96.

19. Ginsborg, Paul, *A History of Contemporary Italy: Society and Politics 1943–88*, Penguin, London, 1990, p. 158. Ginsborg is not specific about the nature of these goods.

20. Milward, Alan S., *The Reconstruction of Western Europe 1945–51*, Methuen, London, 1984, p. 102, quoting US Statistical Abstracts, 1952, pp. 836–7.

21. Ginsborg, Paul, *A History of Contemporary Italy: Society and Politics 1943–88*, Penguin, London, 1990, p. 192.

22. Quoted by Maier, Charles S. (ed.), *The Origins of the Cold War and Contemporary Europe*, New Viewpoints, New York, 1978, p. 13.

23. Hogan, Michael J., *The Marshall Plan: America, Britain and the Reconstruction of Western Europe, 1947–1952*, Cambridge University Press, Cambridge, 1987, p. 443.

24. Ellwood, David, W., *Rebuilding Western Europe, America and Postwar Reconstruction*, Longman, London, 1992, p. 227.

25. Ibid., p. 227.

26. Ginsborg, Paul, *A History of Contemporary Italy: Society and Politics 1943–88*, Penguin, London, 1990, p. 115.

27. Clough, Shephard B., *The Economic History of Modern Italy*, Columbia University Press, 1964, p. 369, quotes the Italian National Annual Statistical Abstract, 1961, p. 437; 'Primi Studi sui Conti Economica Territoriali', p. 137 and the Italian National Annual Statistical Abstract, 1961, p. 401, respectively.

28. Zamagni, Vera, 'American Influence on the Italian Economy 1948–58', in Duggan, Christopher and Duggan, Christopher (eds), *Italy in the Cold War: Politics, Culture and Society 1948–58*, p. 77.

29. Although some large industrial concerns, such as Fiat, knew about American production methods in the inter-war years, there is no evidence that they were implemented on a significant scale until after the Second World War.

30. Zamagni, Vera, 'American Influence on the Italian Economy 1948–58', in Duggan, Christopher and Duggan, Christopher (eds), *Italy in the Cold War: Politics, Culture and Society 1948–58*, p. 82.

31. Ginsborg, Paul, *A History of Contemporary Italy: Society and Politics 1943–88*, Penguin, London, 1990, p. 212. Italy's long-term economic problems include the North-South divide and the lack of natural resources.

32. Ibid., p. 214.

33. The stimulation of the Italian market by deliberate exposure to a mythologised American lifestyle is examined in chapter 4.

34. Micol Fontana in interview, Rome, 23.10.95. Micol Fontana is one of the three sisters who established 'Sorelle Fontana', which was to become one of the most important Italian couture houses in the post-war period.

35. Zamagni, Vera, 'Betting on the Future: the Reconstruction of Italian Industry 1946–52' in Becker, Josef, and Knipping, Franz (eds), *Power in Europe: Great Britain, France, Italy and Germany in a Postwar World 1945–50*, De Gruyter, Berlin and New York, 1986, p. 283.

36. Ginsborg, Paul, *A History of Contemporary Italy: Society and Politics 1943–88*, Penguin, London, 1990, p. 159.

37. Harper, John, *America and the Reconstruction of Italy 1945–8*, Cambridge University Press, 1986, p. 64.

38. Achille Maramotti in interview, Reggio Emilia, 21.7.95.

39. Harper, John, *America and the Reconstruction of Italy 1945–8*, Cambridge University Press, 1986, p. 44.

40. Maramotti interview, Reggio Emilia, 21.7.95.

41. Massai was an economic journalist on the Milan daily newspaper *24 'ore* from 1946 and between 1949–83 reported on Italian fashion for the US trade paper *Women's Wear Daily*. Massai also wrote twice a month for the Milan broadsheet *Corriere della Sera*, on economics, fashion and textiles, between 1967–73. All references to *WWD* are taken from this archive. Important fashion-textile developments between the US and Italy were reported by Massai in the Fairchild trade press, including *WWD* and the *Daily News Record*.

42. Maramotti interview, Reggio Emilia, 21.7.95.

43. Elisa Massai in interview, Milan, 19.7.95.

44. *DNR*, 8.4.60.

45. *WWD*, 8.11.52.

46. Massai, Elisa, 'Italy: 10 Years of Fashion', *WWD*, 1960.

47. For further details see Bull, Anna, Pitt, Martyn and Szarka, Joseph, *Entrepreneurial Textile Communities: A Comparative Study of Small Textile and Clothing Firms*, Chapman & Hall, London, 1993, p. 34.

48. Gianni Ghini in interview, Florence, 17.10.95.

49. Carla Strini in interview, near Florence, 18.10.95.

50. Agache is the only foreign textile manufacturer mentioned by any witness in interview.

51. The Ente Nazionale was the organisation established by the Fascist government to promote the development of Italian fashion and an Italian fashion industry in the interwar period.

2

The Rise of Italian Ready-to-Wear Production

The first collective Italian high fashion show in 1951 is generally hailed as the 'birth of Italian fashion', yet it seems unlikely that an international industry sprang suddenly from nothing. This notion is encapsulated in the title of the exhibition held at the Palazzo Strozzi, 25 June–25 September 1992, entitled 'La Sala Bianca: Nascita della Moda Italiana', which was held to commemorate the 'birth of Italian fashion'. The exhibition was accompanied by a catalogue of the same name, edited by Guido Vergani, and a video produced by VideoCast, Florence. The film contains a mixture of opinions and recollections by historians, PRs and journalists, coupled with original footage of the early Italian fashion shows in Florence, and an interview with Giorgini. La Sala Bianca referred to in the title is the famous 'white room' at the Pitti Palazzo, where the Florentine collections were presented from 1953. The exhibition, catalogue and film were organised by the fashion public relations organisation Pitti Immagine, and were co-ordinated by Luigi Settembrini. In *Italian Metamorphosis 1943–68*, Settembrini writes that 'the birth of Italian fashion can be dated quite precisely as February 12 1951'.[1]

Production Methods up to 1951

Although Italian textile production was industrialised and enjoyed an international market before 1951, the Italian fashion industry was still in an embryonic state. In the more industrially advanced nations, such as the US and Great Britain, large-scale ready-to-wear for women emerged in the mid-to-late nineteenth century. In Italy, even in the immediate post-Second World War years, there was no industrial scale production of fashionable women's ready-to-wear, although off-the-peg mass-produced menswear was already widely available. Certain unfitted items, such as raincoats, had been around for some time, but otherwise women could only buy ready-made clothes on a very small scale, generally from dressmakers. There was little fashionable alternative to made-to-measure.

There were internationally known Italian dress designers working in Italy before the Second World War, such as Fortuny, who was celebrated for his timeless pleated silk robes (patented in 1909), as well as well-known court dressmakers and couturiers, but there was little innovative haute couture in Italy and certainly no significant international market.[2] Nonetheless, there was no shortage of domestic custom for the network of top-level dressmaker salons. This provided a ready market to encourage both excellent craftsmanship in apparel and associated industries and any Italian-based style that might develop.

Italy had long been famous for great craftsmanship. The production of trimmings, fashion embroidery and accessories was already well established through a network of small, elitist manufacturers, especially in the Florence region. There are many surviving examples of the excellent quality of hand-crafted embroidery, such as the floral motif decoration on the bodice and sleeves of a Florentine brown silk two-piece of 1881 in the Pitti Palace collection, shown in figure 2.[3] This tradition did not exist in America and Great Britain, for example. Such embroideries were being exported to the US by the inter-war years. International trade in Italian shoes and leather goods was also expanding in this period, especially with the US. Salvatore Ferragamo is one of the most famous examples.[4] Ferragamo served an apprenticeship in Italy, before establishing a shop in California in 1914, where he attracted the patronage of Hollywood for his hand-made, exclusive designs. He returned to Italy in 1927 and set up in Florence two years later. Whilst in America, he had scrutinised mass production techniques and married industrial and craft production to create highly innovative footwear for the international jet set. Ferragamo's international reputation undoubtedly helped to establish the notion of an Italian fashion industry in the post-war years. Moreover, the long tradition of fine Italian dressmakers and pattern makers (many of whom were employed by Paris houses) was well known in the US and a number of the leading tailors in New York and in Hollywood costume had Italian names, such as Casella and D'Andrea.

In *1922–1943 Vent'Anni di Moda Italiana*, Italian dress historian Grazietta Butazzi has described how the Fascist creed of autarky (1932–43) had a significant effect on the confidence of Italian dressmakers.[5] Many of the high fashion names mentioned in the Italian press in the early 1940s were those who acquired international reputations in the post-war period, including: Noberasko, Villa, Gabriella Sport, Ferrario, Fercioni, Vanna, San Lorenzo, Simonetta, Fabiani, Pucci and Marucelli. None of this activity was on an industrial scale and cannot be said to constitute a new international Italian fashion industry, but it highlighted both individual and collective aptitude and pointed towards future success. In the war years, Italian fashion production

Figure 2. Brown silk two-piece gown, with heavily embroidered bodice and sleeves. Made in Tuscany,1881. Label reads 'G. Giabbani/Sarta'. Source: Pitti Palace, Florence, TA 1913, n.1806. Courtesy of the Ministero per i Beni e le Attività Culturali. Further reproductions or duplications by any means are forbidden.

continued and those involved developed a new awareness of the sector's potential, through increased self-sufficiency. At this pivotal moment for Italian fashion, before the expansion of the international trade, it is clear that Italian clients formed the important market. Since Paris haute couture was unavailable during the war years, the Italian upper classes became more used to patronising Italian designers, and continued to do so in the immediate post-war years. This wartime Italian custom was crucial to the success of Italian fashion designers in the post-war period, because it enabled them to establish a secure position, and to take advantage of the international market when it emerged in the late 1940s; couturier Micol Fontana clearly states that 'we started in Rome with the Italian aristocracy'.

By the immediate post-war period, there were two identifiable types of elite dressmaking establishment in Italy. The first was of artisan origin, such as Sorelle Fontana, Fabiani, and Antonelli, whilst designers in the second group came from the higher social echelons, mostly young women from the aristocracy and upper middle classes, many of whom were suffering financial difficulties as a result of war and saw new personal and financial opportunities in fashion. This category includes names such as Marchese Pucci, Princess Caracciolo (Carosa), Marchesa de Gresy (Mirsa) and Simonetta Visconti. They may have lacked technical knowledge, but they were seen as elegant, sophisticated and refined and traded on their sophisticated notion of exclusive Italian 'good taste'. However, both categories continued to operate on a small scale, from craft-oriented workshops.

Italy's reputation for artisanal excellence recuperated swiftly after the War and with it, her export trade in craft-based goods. Florence had been the traditional centre of Italian craftsmanship since the early twentieth century and consequently was the centre of Italian exports. It was also the centre of the buying offices for foreign markets, the largest of which was the US. In the immediate post-war years, many Italian goods, especially handicrafts, such as linens, ceramics, infant knits, straw-work and small leather goods sold increasingly well in America. The precise testimony of Enzo Tayar offers a reliable explanation of this development.[6]

Tayar became a buyer of Italian goods for the US market in the inter-war period. In 1913, his father had become manager of Roditi and Sons Buying Office in Florence and was one of the first Florentine buyers to do business with the US. Prior to the War Tayar organised the export of handicrafts to the US: ironwork, straw, embroideries, and other 'artistic' crafts. He explains that buyers arrived by boat from the US and typically spent one or two months travelling Europe on each trip. During the War the market shifted to South America, but in 1945, as the European markets re-opened, Tayar and his father re-opened the Roditi buying office in Florence. Almost immediately there was a 'tremendous influx of buying trade', especially Americans looking for new artefacts. Tayar took his first buying trip to the US in 1945 and claims that he was the first and only one, at this time. He travelled to New York on a 'Victory Ship', because as yet he says, there were no planes flying. He took with him forty-five cases of Italian handicraft samples of 'all the things that Italy used to sell prior to the War, embroideries, leather goods, ceramics and so on'. Tayar stayed in the US for six months and 'did a lot of business', including a big trade show in New York.

From this point, US buyers came to Italy in large numbers by plane. Tayar and his brother Frank went into business by themselves in 1949, in a one-room office in Florence, with one employee, specifically to take advantage of the expanding US trade. Although the goods, mostly accessories, were still produced at artisan level, they were accompanied by potent advertising campaigns and, encouraged by the US market, were increasingly styled for US requirements. This is confirmed in an article entitled 'Jury chooses Italian Ceramics for Brooklyn Museum Exhibit', which was published by *RD* (Fairchild Publications) in May 1950. The article describes the preparations for an exhibition due to start in November 1950, which was to tour twelve other museums in the US. All items were purchased in Italy by the Brooklyn museum and were for sale at the exhibition. The famous US industrial designer, Walter Dorwin Teague, was part of the selecting committee, and said that 'most of the articles we have chosen have not yet been shown in Europe. The trip convinced the experts that Italian artisans, if properly directed, can reduce their prices and cater successfully to American tastes.' At this point, a government-sponsored organisation for the development of handicrafts for export to the US was established under the name of Compagnia Nazionale Artigiana (CNP). A permanent showroom for CNP products was established in New York and as *WWD* explained in June 1955, 'although there was some criticism of the program (sic), the CNP did much to make the American public aware of what Italy had to offer, and Italian craftsmen informed about the American market'.

In addition, a few Italian accessory firms, such as the shoe designer Ferragamo (who had already won the prestigious US Neiman Marcus award by 1947) were forging international reputations in specialised fashion fields. At this stage, knitwear was not yet seen by the contemporary press as part of mainstream fashion, but as part of 'handicrafts', albeit fashion-related. Although knit was not a significant export straight after the War, according to *WWD* (June 1955), top quality knit 'soon came into the program, and as early as 1947 Luisa Spagnoli was exporting angora knits to the US'. The first *WWD* story devoted to formal Italian silk knitwear for the high fashion market, appeared in June 1950. According to a later report (February 1956), this story encouraged the production of formal silk-knit separates in the Milan area, by companies such as Avagolf, Madil and others.

As a result of all this American interest in Italy's traditional craft/fashion skills, it was perhaps natural for any developing Italian fashion manufacture to gravitate towards the US market. Indeed, in November 1960, Fairchild published an article entitled *Italy: Ten Years of Fashion*, by Elisa Massai, which gives a fascinating overview of the crucial early post-war evolution of Italian fashion production from its craft roots. Massai had worked as a correspondent for Fairchild since 1948, and in this key article, Massai recalled that 'in the late 1940s, the idea of Italian fashion started to take place through an awareness of Italian creative and artisanal potential. The international reputation of Italy's highly skilled craftsmanship and textiles had already been established.'

In 1948, Franco Marinotti, President of rayon company Snia Viscosa, established the Italian Fashion Centre (*Centro Italiana della Moda*). For Marinotti, the anticipated advantage was that the use of rayon by top dressmakers would gain respect for Italian-produced artificial fibres. For the dressmakers, it provided the support of an official organisation which aimed to 'concentrate the scattered initiatives of individual dressmakers in a single national fashion fair that would facilitate the task of fashion writers and buyers' and would help to establish them on the international fashion scene.[7] This is another clear example of the central role played by the Italian textile industry within the development processes of the Italian fashion industry. According to *WWD* (March 1950), the shows were held in Venice in conjunction with the Film Festival, in order to attract a foreign audience, and included most of the big dressmakers of Milan, Rome and Florence, who were to become famous in the next decade, names such as Biki, Marucelli, Veneziani, Curiel, Tizzoni, Fercioni, Galitzine, Capucci, and Baratta. The presentations were reinforced by official receptions for the foreign buyers.

There are also a number of reported examples of Italian fashion designers selling in America in the immediate post-war years. Two of the earliest to come to US attention were Simonetta and Emilio Pucci. *Sunday Times* fashion journalist Ernestine Carter recalls in her autobiography that 'Rome had been the first to catch fashion eyes when Simonetta opened her shop in 1946' and that she hit 'the international scene when American *Vogue* photographed her, her sister, and her mother and a friend, all beautiful, and all wearing evening dresses by Simonetta'.[8] Evidently, a certain international kudos was beginning to envelop Italian fashion very soon after the War ended.

Pucci studied in the US during the inter-war period and produced his first 'collection' there, for his college uniform. An Olympic skier in the interwar years, Pucci found himself in hard times after the War and began to produce a line of top quality colourful leisure outfits and sandals for friends. Following the discovery of his designs in St Moritz by a *Harper's Bazaar* photographer in 1947 they were reproduced by 'White Stag' sportswear of Portland, Oregon, for Lord and Taylor and were displayed in their 5th Avenue windows. At $39.95 for the ski-pants, this was very expensive ready-to-wear, but nonetheless the range was featured in *Harper's Bazaar* in December 1948 and praised for its comfort and elegance, if not its economy. The brightly coloured prints and tight stretchy trousers were an almost instant success.

Pucci's production was still small-scale, representing only a fraction of the international sales he achieved in the 1950s and 1960s, and cannot be said to constitute a universal trend. Nonetheless, he was undoubtedly famous in US fashion circles by the end of the 1940s and his success pointed firmly to future developments, in terms of both style and production. Pucci was 'discovered' and promoted by the US and, encouraged by his sources within the American retail trade, instantly began to move towards higher volume manufacture in Italy, whilst preserving his 'quality' status.

Elisa Massai, writing in *WWD* in November 1960, charts other links between other Italian designers and the US market which developed quickly from this point: 'During the 1947–1950 period stores like Marshall Field, Lord and Taylor, and Hudson's had already contacted a handful of couture designers from Simonetta to Fontana of Rome and from Biki to Marucelli and Veneziani of Milan.' In an earlier piece, Massai specified that 'J.L. Hudson and company was probably the first store to publicise Italian clothes, in 1949.' Massai clearly viewed this as the germination period of Italian fashion, and quoted export figures to the US, published by the Italian Central Statistical Institute for 'sewn goods' (including ready-to-wear for men, women and children, as well as lingerie, beachwear, ties, rainwear, and scarves) of $595,283 for 1950, plus $364,741 of knitwear (mainly men's socks and women's hosiery).[9] These were relatively small sums, but they are notable because they represent the roots of the post-war success of Italian fashion.

In March 1950, *WWD* published its first three reports on the Italian 'fashion showings for Spring', 'in view of the American trade interest in the Italian style market'. Over three weeks, the extensive reports assessed the state of Italian fashion production in Milan, Florence and Rome in relation to the American market. Significantly, the writer was clear that although 'there is practically no high-style ready-to-wear in this part of the world', several Italian high fashion houses were already promoting themselves actively to the American market. Both Bellenghi and Fantechi of Florence took 'their collections to Rome each season so that Americans coming to Italy and not going to Florence have the opportunity to see them in the capital city'. Furthermore, the article stressed that 'Fontana (of Rome) has had considerable publicity in the US because it has dressed a number of well-known American movie stars. Fontana clothes have a professional look, well-made, well-presented, even in an informal advance showing of a few typical models which the sisters were kind enough to stage for *WWD*.'

It is clear that a number of crucial strands in the post-war flowering of Italian fashion can already be identified by 1951. These strands include Italy's reputation for quality dressmaking, embroidery and accessories, the active pursuit of Italian-made garments by the US fashion trade, and the active pursuit of the American market by Italian dressmakers. It is also clear that no high fashion women's ready-to-wear industry had been established in Italy before the first collective high fashion shows in 1951.

The Early Development of US Ready-to-wear as a Model for Italian Production

The mass-production of women's ready-to-wear in America formed a key model for the development of the Italian fashion industry in the 1945–65 period. In the US, as in the other more industrially advanced Western nations, fashionable women's ready-to-wear production had begun in the mid-nineteenth century. The evolution of the American ready-to-wear industry is well known.[10] Ready-made clothing for women was fully accepted in the US by 1920, significantly earlier than in Europe, where it retained a low-status image for the higher social groups for some years.[11] For example, in 1910, the magazine *Home Life in America* published the commentary of a Mrs Katherine Busbey, who remarked that it was undoubtedly possible for the middle class to dress far better and cheaper in America, than abroad, because 'the ready-made suit in the American shop is comparatively better cut than those for the same price in European markets'.[12]

The role of European immigrant workers in the swift development of the American wholesale clothing trade cannot be underestimated. A significant number of them had experience in tailoring and related trades, and many others provided unskilled labour. The 'great migration' from eastern and southern Europe came between 1880–1920, and coincided with the greatest growth in the American ready-made clothing industry. The Italian immigration began in 1890, increasing swiftly from 1900 and many of the immigrants were already accomplished dressmakers. Although the first of this group were Polish and Russian Jews, by the early twentieth century, Italian women dominated the garment industry. During the 1920s, they became the single largest group in the clothing sector, displacing the Jews, and by 1937, immigrant and second-generation Italians numbered 100,000 out of 250,000 (workers) in the New York area.[13] These workers were later to assume a vital role in communications between the Italian and American fashion industries.

By the outbreak of the Second World War, wearing ready-made clothing had become customary for almost all American women. Even the very rich were buying off-the-peg everyday wear, albeit of a very different quality to that worn by the poor, as American economist Paul Nystrom wrote in 1928: 'the processes of standardisation have gone far toward providing much more than a majority of the population with well-fitted factory garments.[14] This can be qualified by the contents of American women's magazines; even US

Vogue carried numerous ready-to-wear advertisements and editorials. In January 1935, for example, Dupont Rayon advertised a range of ready-to-wear summer garments available from US department stores. This included a buttoned dress with polka dot scarf which was sold in Lord and Taylor's 'sportswear' department in sizes 14 to 42 for $17.95.

By this time, the manufacturing process was flexibly structured and allowed for both handwork and assembly-line production. Machines could cut hundreds of layers at once, and produce thousands of stitches per minute. Distribution could reach everyone, and there was an extensive mass-market with some disposable income; all the elements for successful mass production were in place. Probably the most important ingredient in the success of American fashion manufacture was the complexity of the market levels within ready-to-wear production, which included high quality garments produced by well-known designers such as Hattie Carnegie (who was one of the very first to design and produce her own range of ready-to-wear, under her own label, in the 1930s). The key to this seems to have been threefold: discovering exactly what the market wanted, producing it on a large scale using the latest machinery, and selling it hard. With an almost unlimited production capacity, it made sense to stimulate change. Once the Second World War was over, America was in a position not only to sell its products internationally, but also to teach these lessons to other nations. Moreover, although American manufacture catered for all levels of the ready-to-wear market, there was no large-scale production at the top end, and as this market expanded in the post-war years, a niche was revealed, which Italy was well placed to fill.

The US Response to the First Collective Italian Fashion Shows

On 12 February 1951, the first international collective fashion show was staged in Italy and it remains one of the most well-documented aspects of Italian fashion history. The show was organised by Giovan Battista Giorgini at his own home, the splendid Villa Torrignani in Florence. Giorgini had been a 'commissionaire' of craft goods for US department stores (including big names such as Magnin) in the inter-war and immediate post-war years. In fact, for the Americans, he was one of the top two Florentine buyers. Significantly, the idea for the show came when Giorgini was returning from a business trip to the US, which underlines the fact that it was prompted by his dealings with and understanding of, the requirements of the American market. Initially funding the show himself, Giorgini set about persuading Italian designers as well as the US stores and journalists, to take part.

Initially, only a few couture designers and stores agreed. They were: Carosa, Simonetta, Schuberth, Fontana (Rome), and Veneziani, Vanna, Noberasko and Marucelli (Milan). Some 'Boutique' level designers such as Pucci and

Tessitrice of Capri, who produced high-quality, ready-to-wear sportswear, also showed. In a contemporary interview, Giorgini explained that 'it took me nearly all year and I travelled frequently to Milan and Rome and other Italian cities to contact the new fashion houses. Finally I put together ten of them, each of which was supposed to give me eighteen outfits. I intended to show them at the start of 1951, since Paris was showing in the first week of February. I hoped to persuade the buyers from the American companies that I represented to come from Florence to Paris.'[15]

Over three days they showed approximately 180 models to representatives of Giorgini's American clients: Altmans and Bergdorfs of New York, Magnins of San Francisco, Morgans of Montreal, as well as two US ready-to-wear manufacturers, Leto Cohn Lo Balbo, and Hannah Troy.[16] This made up the total of eight individual buyers. Gianni Ghini, who helped Giorgini organise the shows from 1952, remembers that the latter two attended 'by accident', because they 'bumped into' the store buyers in a Florence street, on their way to the show, and were invited along. At this stage there was no 'entrance fee', as there was at the Paris shows, whereby every buyer had to pay a 'deposit' which was returnable upon purchase. Although there were a number of Italian reporters, Elisa Massai, of *WWD*, was the only journalist representing a foreign publication, at the first show. The evening was an absolute success, the buyers bought well and the journalists reported favourably, as Giorgini explained: 'this group of American buyers (and they were important names), went back to America with such enthusiasm that when I held the second runway presentation, some three hundred came over from America, including buyers and press'.[17] Elisa Massai defines the significance of the occasion thus: 'the great change occurred in February 1951, and US interest began to burgeon from that point on'.[18]

The low cost of Italian fashion was evidently crucial to eliciting American interest at this stage, especially in comparison to rising French prices. In January 1952, *WWD* explained that 'prices vary greatly, starting at the equivalent of $100 or less at some houses, and seldom exceeding $400, with the exception of richly embroidered gowns. Retail buyers are said to be satisfied with the prices'. These prices were reported to be 'well under richly embroidered gowns shown elsewhere'. This referred precisely to Paris, and the difference was further stressed in another report later that year, under the heading 'Prices half those of France'. Moreover, prices for Italian boutique fashions were significantly lower than the couture. As *WWD* stated in 1952, Italian couture ranged 'from $130–250 for daytime, to $120–500 for evening, while resort or boutique clothes shown are around $90–130'.

It is highly significant that already, the most successful of the Italian collections were in the boutique category. Early press reports pointed firmly towards future developments. In September 1951, Italian fashion magazine *Novità* wrote that 'the biggest purchases by the Americans were made in these [boutique] collections, and we truly think that the future of Italian fashion lies precisely in sportswear'. *Novità* advised that Italian fashion should 'offer clothes that, although equal to the French, will be completely different, focusing on simplicity, high quality materials, and cut'.

As the only foreign journalist present, Massai was the first to report the Italian show in the international press, on the front page of *WWD*, 14 February 1951, in a famous piece entitled 'Italian styles gain approval of US buyers'. The second show was covered by a major article in *Life*, the biggest American mass-market periodical, under the headline 'Italy gets dressed up: a big, hectic fashion show attracts US style leaders, poses a challenge to Paris'. The text was accompanied by several location shots of the designs, as well as the designers pictured with Giorgini, and one of the show itself. Such publicity was often misleading. Paris was clearly not under threat at this point, yet with such widespread positive coverage, numbers continued to grow and the show was forced to move again in January 1953, to the impressive Sala Bianca at the Pitti Palace. By this stage, the presentation was spread over five days, with 350 spectators and sixteen boutique designers who showed alongside the couture and it was firmly placed in the international fashion circuit.

In January 1955, Giorgini resigned his position as organiser of the shows, as a result of rivalries between the fashion centres of Rome and Florence, which both wanted to be known as 'the fashion capital of Italy'. However, the Florentine event was clearly well established in the international market by this time, and the shows continued without him. Two years later, in May 1957, *WWD* announced that 'The Italian couture has decided to stand together and show in Florence, thus ending the fashion feud with Rome.' The return of Roman designers Simonetta, Fabiani, Capucci and Carosa to the Florentine fold was seen as 'the best way to strengthen Italian design and expand model sales to American and European stores and manufacturers'. Expansion remained the central aim, and for the time being these designers were prepared to compromise in order to attain it.

This aim was achieved on an impressive scale and the volume of Italian clothes sold abroad increased dramatically. *WWD* coverage supports the notion that the Florence shows stimulated an export boom; in June 1955, for example, Massai reported that Giorgini's 'idea has boomed Italian exports for the last five years'. Furthermore, Elisa Massai's archive contains a table of Italian exports and imports, including key statistics which reveal the extent of the expansion. Women's and children's clothing exports rose by 500 per cent, from a value of L45,327 in 1950, to L226,617 five years later.[19] These figures were not composed entirely of made-to-measure clothing and rising volume production was clearly a vital factor in the dramatic increase.

The Role of the US Market in the Move Towards Serial Production

Traditionally, the official international appearance of Italian ready-to-wear fashion is dated at 1975, when the first collective international presentation of Italian 'prêt-à-porter' (high fashion ready-to-wear) began in Milan. More recent assessments suggest that it began slightly earlier, in 1972, when a number of prêt-à-porter designers began showing independently in Milan.[20] However, it is evident that crucial developments in this direction, in terms of mass-production and exports, took place considerably earlier. Their roots can be traced back as far as the early 1950s. High fashion was exported in significant quantities, mainly to the US, at both couture and boutique levels from 1951, following the collective presentations organised by Giorgini.[21] Whilst couture output increased considerably in the 1950s, boutique output, which was made ready-to-wear, expanded even more impressively and by the late 1950s, quality Italian ready-to-wear was being exported to the US in significant quantities.

Volume Purchases of Italian High Fashion by US Stores   Thus from 1951, US department stores purchased Italian high fashion enthusiastically, and in increasing volume. Through his pivotal role in the Florence shows, Gianni Ghini has an almost unique understanding of the relationship between the US market and the designers who showed collectively in Florence and is able to describe it in detail. He explains that 'from the very beginning, the Americans had the lion's share of the sales'.[22] This is perhaps not surprising, considering the extent of the US market for clothing and the fact that in the immediate post-war years, American stores vied with each other to tap fresh overseas markets for goods to sell in the US. *WWD* coverage reveals that most US department stores sent representatives to the Italian collections within a year or two of their inauguration. By 1952 they included J.W. Robinson, Marshall Field, Kaufmann, Gump, and Jordan Marsh, as well as the more famous elite stores such as Bergdorf Goodman.

Conversely, although other nations such as Britain, sent buyers, they were in small numbers, and bought relatively little, hampered by exchange difficulties. At this point, according to Ghini, American stores were each spending, typically, around $10,000 per annum on Italian 'high fashion', (including haute couture and boutique level). This was a lot of money and naturally, Ghini says, 'everyone was delighted'. US store buyers continued to attend the couture collections in large numbers and there is no evidence in the detailed statistics offered by *WWD* that sales of Italian couture to the US market tailed off during the 1951–65 period.

Although the first shows were free, by 1953 a system of entrance deposits, or 'cautions', had been introduced, whereby each buyer paid a mandatory $100 entrance fee in return for coupons which could be set against the purchase of models. This was a significant amount in Italy, which Ghini equates to over two months salary for an Italian clerk, or the cost of a simple haute couture dress or suit, but was considerably less than was charged for the same system at the Paris shows and therefore did nothing to discourage the US market. This is verified by *WWD* coverage, which in January 1952, for example, stated that 'Simonetta and Fabiani have attracted the largest buyer contingent so far, despite the fact that they are the only ones to demand an entrance deposit.' By 1963, deposits had risen to $250, against Paris charges of '$800 and up', according to *WWD*, in February 1963. Furthermore, the cost of Italian models was approximately 'half those of France' (*WWD* July 1952).

The testimony of couturier Micol Fontana, of Sorelle Fontana, who showed at the first presentation in 1951, presents a key example of one Italian designer's trade relationship with the US market, from the couturier's perspective. Commenting on the significance of the US market, she says that 'Fontana sold a lot to the US stores, from the beginning, and this was an important market for us. From the late 1950s, Saks was our best store client, and would take a considerable range of our designs every season.' According to Fontana, this experience was typical of most of the couture trade between US stores and Italian designers.

Furthermore, almost from the very start of the formal presentation of Italian fashion, many of the Italian designers who took part made sales agreements with US stores. These were on a variety of levels, from exclusive sale of entire couture collections to individual stores, to the right to copy or translate particular designs. Simonetta, for example, sold her entire spring 1951 couture collection to Bergdorf Goodman, whilst many designers sold only to one or two particular stores under both formal and informal arrangements. Such an arrangement might mean, for example, that a designer would sell to only one store in California, and one in New York. More significantly, most designers sold the right to reproduce their creations.

Sales for Reproduction by US Department Stores and Manufacturers From the 1950s, the most exclusive US stores such as Bergdorf Goodman, Saks, Neiman Marcus and Altman were all spending a few thousand dollars on buying for reproduction (copying or translation) as well as the designs they bought for resale. The less expensive stores such as Ohrbach, generally bought only for copying and translation.[23] This meant that they would have the designs copied or translated by ready-to-wear manufacturers on New York's Seventh Avenue, to sell in their own outlets. The stores also often bought the relevant Italian fabric from the textile producer linked to the selected Italian fashion designer, for their own versions, which indicates that the promotional tie-ins described in chapter 1 were successful.

Moreover, it is apparent in *WWD* coverage, that from 1951 US ready-to-wear manufacturers (predominantly from Seventh Avenue), came to Italy in increasing numbers to buy both boutique and couture designs for translation and 'volume reproduction'. What is of great significance here, and justifies the financial patronage of Italian fashion by the Italian textile industry, is that they also customarily bought the fabrics from the 'linked' Italian textile producers. US ready-to-wear manufacturers were an increasingly important market for Italian designers at the Florence shows, and this continued into the 1960s. After the Americans, the British were the most important manufacturing market. The American involvement at this level started at the very first show, attended by Hannah Troy and Leto Cohn Lo Balbo, whilst Ben Zuckerman and David Zelinka (of Seventh Avenue) were the biggest new ready-to-wear names at the third show, although Ghini stresses that there were 'many others'. An example of this relationship can be seen in figure 3, a Fabiani cape-coat made in 'super shaggy fleece' which was copied by US manufacturer Swansdown for $110, photographed at St Peter's, Rome and advertised in *Life* magazine in August 1951.

These US manufacturers were directly demonstrating the possibilities of volume production to the Italian designers, generally for the first time. In the case of Micol Fontana, for example, the experience had a marked effect. On her first visit to New York, in 1951, Fontana recalls the powerful impact of both the retail opportunities of 5th Avenue, and the ready-to-wear capacity of 7th Avenue, and describes it as 'very exciting, a big experience'. Whilst the significance of such ad hoc encounters is difficult to define, it is clear that they contributed to Italian understanding of the size and strength of the industrialised US fashion system. Furthermore, as an important market, the requirements of US ready-to-wear companies were becoming crucial to the Italian designers, and they responded positively to the US calls for volume output.

Volume Sales of Ready-Made 'Boutique'   There were a few Italian high-fashion designers, such as Pucci, who never designed couture, but instead began with very high-quality ready-to-wear, or 'boutique' production, in the immediate post-war years. Such garments were presented at the special 'boutique' collections which accompanied the couture showings from the

Figure 3. Fabiani cape-coat in 'super shaggy fleece', photographed at St Peter's, Rome. Copies of this garment were available from US ready-to-wear manufacturer Swansdown at $110 retail. Source: *Life*, 20.8.51, p. 106. Courtesy of The Archives of Milton H. Greene, LLC.

beginning. Boutique designs were generally less formal than the couture, and centred on elite casual daywear. Prices were much lower than couture, and by July 1956, averaged 'between $10–40 per garment', against average couture prices 'from $160–500, with 30–40 per cent less for models by young designers', and were sold in greater quantities, according to *WWD*. At first, both the store and manufacturing buyers purchased more couture than boutique, because this was their traditional purchase, and also because the couture made up the bulk of the garments shown. According to Ghini, the early attitude of the buyers to boutique was that it was 'amusing', but not as 'safe' a market as the couture, and not very important to the industry. However, 'very soon they were buying it enthusiastically'.[24]

As we have seen, Emilio Pucci is known as the earliest Italian designer to achieve success in the international market in the post-war period, and remains one of the best-known Italian designers. His is also probably the earliest example of boutique level production in Italy (from 1948), and although there is no evidence that his designs were being officially translated by US manufacturers so early on, he offers a relevant case study in two ways. Firstly, Pucci made numerous deals with US stores for the sale of his designs, and his activities can be seen as a key example of a boutique designer selling entire collections to individual stores. Secondly, Pucci's production grew from craft-based beginnings with the help of this strong international market, and is in many respects a typical example of changing working methods in Italian boutique level fashion.

Although Pucci's contribution to international fashion has been assessed in some detail, there is still little scholarly analysis of his dealings with America.[25] However, the details can be pieced together through assessment of Fairchild press coverage and the recollections of Carla Strini. Strini was 'Head of Foreign Operations' at Pucci in the mid-1950s, when Pucci's international reputation was still being established and is able to offer a uniquely detailed description of Pucci's working methods and his international operations.

The US represented the bulk of his market, with Italy, England, Belgium and Switzerland making up the remainder; by the late 1950s, there were still no outlets in France. The US press devoted an increasing amount of eulogistic attention to Pucci from 1947 onwards. Because Pucci's garments were at the very top end of ready-to-wear, his sales were almost entirely to the top department stores. The most consistently important were Neiman Marcus, Saks, Lord and Taylor and Bonwit Teller in the US and Woolands in the UK. Prices in the US were very high for ready-to-wear. For example, in *Pucci: a Renaissance in Fashion*, Shirley Kennedy states that a Pucci dress cost $190 at a New York store in 1963, which equates to the lower end of Italian couture prices. The target market was ladies who traditionally wore couture and who saw Pucci's garments as suitably chic but not expensive.

Strini was responsible for sales agreements with the stores, and recalls arranging both formal and informal deals. Sometimes a 'gentleman's agreement' would be reached to sell a particular collection to a store, but for any form of exclusivity a formal contract had to be signed. 'Exclusivity' in this context broadly meant the unique right to sell a particular collection in a particular country or city. It was also possible, for example, for Neiman Marcus in Texas and Saks in New York to receive the same designs (provided the stores agreed), but whilst the cut and fabric pattern could be the same, the colours never were. Exclusivity was marked by special labels which were woven in Italy and exported with the garments. According to Strini, 'the label was an official recognition of an exclusivity agreement'. There are a number of surviving examples of these labels in American museum collections, which typically, for example, read 'An exclusive Emilio design for Saks 5th Avenue'.[26]

Generally the contracts were yearly, covering two collections, but could be extended, and often were. Woolands, for example, maintained their contract for at least three years in the mid-1950s, giving them exclusivity in London. Saks first signed with Pucci in 1954, and at that point shared the right to sell Pucci's collection in America with Lord and Taylor (in different colourways) on a 60:40 basis. Strini states that 'Saks' purchasing power was enormous'; they represented an extremely good market for Pucci designs throughout the period under study, and effectively had 'first choice'. A Saks buyer typically travelled to Florence four or five times each year to buy Pucci, Strini recalls. Furthermore, there is firm evidence in the pages of *WWD* that Pucci was involved in at least one deal with a New York ready-to-wear manufacturer. In April 1957, it reported that Pucci was shortly to arrive in New York 'to design a sweater collection for Darlene', which was to be manufactured and distributed in the US. By 1963, Pucci's export business was reputed to be worth over $500,000, mainly in America, although by this stage the label was sold in fifty-nine countries.[27]

Yet within these expanding sales, exclusivity remained crucial to Pucci's financial success, and understanding this, he refused to retail ever more widely. In the late 1950s, for example, Sackowitz of Houston asked Pucci to sell to them, but as he told Gianni Ghini at the time, he refused, saying 'I have to protect my name in this way.' Although he licensed many products, from shoes to perfume, Pucci was not tempted to sell his garment designs for industrial reproduction and he did not produce in sufficient quantities to target the extensive American mass market. Nevertheless, Pucci's initial decision to produce ready-to-wear rather than couture, albeit by traditional methods at high fashion level, can be firmly related to his early experience of the US market. His years in the US equipped him with some understanding of the American market, and the possibilities of elite ready-to-wear production.

During this period, *WWD* reported increasingly intense US interest in Italian boutique production, saying in February 1955 that 'producers of boutique clothes are still very busy with spring deliveries, and Bertoli of Milan, for example, has again had to postpone his trip to the US because of pressure for deliveries'. By December 1956 the same paper was able to list a throng of Italian boutique houses who were showing at the Florentine presentations, and which were said to be 'already familiar to American buyers', including Avolio, Bertoli, Myricae, Valditevere, Vito and Giara d'Arno, together with two new names, Adria of Rome and Gianni Baldini of Portofino. Significantly, this 1956 report also included the first reference to boutique house collections created especially for the American market: 'Emilio, Mirsa, Glans and Avagolf have designed, for American buyers, special ranges of daytime suits and coats, as well as outstanding separates for resort or sport and knitwear from Mirsa and Avagolf.'

Unfortunately, the exact quantities commissioned are not known, but at this point, *WWD* (November 1956) reported that in 'Portofino, fresh Italian playwear source', Gianni Baldini, for example, was producing sportswear for 'wholesale prices ranging from $4.50–11, for a minimum of a dozen, first cost (wholesale)', indicating a significant rise in production capacity of fashionable ready-to-wear. This 'ready-to-wear collection of printed cotton skirts, slacks, pants, dresses and beachcoats' was 'reported successful with leading US stores'. In January 1957, American retail interest in Italian sports-wear was said to be 'reaching unexpected levels, as illustrated by export figures for 1956, which register about $22 million for merchandise to the US, in comparison with $15 million in 1955, and $2 million in 1950.' These figures included 'knit, sports and beach wear, and fashion accessories' and show a massive eleven-fold increase in the US market for Italian high-quality ready-mades, over the six years 1950–6. There is little reference in *WWD* to any other export market than the US, although Germany and Britain begin to be mentioned towards the end of the 1950s.

Ready-to-Wear Production by Italian Couturiers   High-quality ready-to-wear was not however solely the domain of 'boutique' designers. All 'designer ready-to-wear' was known collectively as boutique and by the late 1950s clothing of this type was also produced by most of the Italian couturiers too, cashing in on this new target market. Probably the earliest 'boutique' collec-tion produced by an Italian couturier was Gattinoni's, presented at the Florence collections in 1952. There was a gradual expansion into this area by most of the other designers, which quickened in the late 1950s. By 1961, these included Antonelli, Simonetta, Veneziani, Guidi, Marucelli, Biki, Mingolini-Guggenheim, Galitzine, De Luca, Schuberth, Fontana and Capucci.

At first, the manufacture of these lines was generally undertaken by Italian ready-to-wear manufacturers operating under licence. Antonelli's, for example, was manufactured by Comber ready-to-wear of Vicenza in 1956. However, very significantly, by the end of the decade, couturiers such as Fontana began to set up their own factories for the production of boutique level ready-to-wear. Fontana's boutique label, established in 1960, was called 'Fontana Alta-Moda-Pronta'. It was designed by the Fontana sisters, and produced in a new factory just outside Rome, which employed 400 people. As Micol

Fontana remembers, this was not a large operation by American standards, but it was for Italy, especially at this quality level. The collection was created specifically 'for the American market', and Micol Fontana explains that they often sold lines to the US stores on an exclusive basis. It was distributed to 100 shops in America, compared to 70 in Italy, and only 30 in England. However, it is significant that an aura of made-to-measure was carefully and cleverly maintained. Fontana says that 'the exclusive deals with individual stores for the prêt-à-porter collections, included personal selection of trimmings, such as buttons, by the store representatives'.

Even more significantly, Fontana had already directly experienced designing for ready-to-wear production, three years previously, in America. In 1957, a 7th Avenue manufacturer called Tafel approached them to design a high fashion 'morning-through-til-night' collection to be retailed in America, in the big stores. Fontana remarks that 'this gave me a curiosity about ready-to-wear techniques and made me want to learn more'. Precisely how many other high fashion designers had their first direct experiences of ready-to-wear production in conjunction with the US ready-to-wear industry in this way is not known, but there are certainly other important examples of exclusive collections for the US market, including Schuberth's 1960 collection.[28]

Furthermore, the American market gave the Fontana sisters their first experience of diversification, when Micol designed both stockings and shoes to be sold there under licence, in 1962. In this case the initiative came from the US manufacturer, who approached Fontana with the idea. The deal led to many other licences for all sorts of accessory products, and perfume.[29] Whilst accessories remain peripheral to the main clothing market, all these examples indicate that Italian high fashion designers were being tempted into experiencing mass-production by US manufacturers, although this does not necessarily mean that they would use that knowledge to replicate the American system exactly.

The Italian boutique trade continued to expand throughout the 1950s and the collections were applauded loudly in the US trade press. As early as August 1951, for example, following the second Florentine presentation, *WWD* used a full page of illustrations to reinforce their suggestion that 'inventive Italian boutique items' by Pucci, Bertoli, Simonetta and Veneziani 'could be peaked for main floor merchandising'. This suggests that the press were already confident that Italian boutique would appeal to department store clientele in the USA. In 1956, trade was still booming, and *WWD* recorded that 'according to reports of commissionaires and resident buying offices, business last January was brightest ever'. By May 1960, sales were continuing to expand at a heady rate, and under the headline 'US buyer peak due for Italy; sales up 10–20 per cent: many stores set big promotions', *WWD* stated that 'more Americans are visiting the Italian market than ever before, they are coming earlier, and they are buying in greater depth'.

In January 1957, in an article entitled 'US record set on Sportswear buying in Italy', *WWD* had spoken of heavy sales to top retailers such as Neiman Marcus, mass-market stores such as Filene and Ohrbach, as well as 7th Avenue manufacturers such as Frank Gallant, Arthur Jablow and Ben Zuckerman. It also announced that Simonetta's boutique collection 'sold at wholesale', had been 'given in exclusivity for California to I. Magnin, and for Texas to Neiman Marcus. Lord and Taylor are expected to have exclusivity of it for New York and Boston.' This was reported as a 'normal' event, which indicates that similar deals to those arranged by Carla Strini for Pucci, were the norm in boutique level production.

By December 1959, a number of further developments in the move towards volume sales were noted by *WWD*. Firstly, Antonelli was producing 'a dozen models prepared specially for ready-to-wear manufacturers for reproduction in fall lines'. Secondly, the journal stated that 'Carosa, one of the last Italian houses to remain solely haute couture, has concluded arrangements with two Italian ready-to-wear manufacturers, one in Sicily, one in Lombardy to supply models for reproduction. The wholesale price will be $60–110 from the Sicily factory; the Lombardy one will produce a cheaper range' and thirdly, 'Bonwit Teller has been so successful with Simonetta's playsuits, selling here for $11–12, that she is now studying ways to mass-produce this item here [USA] at a cheaper price'. Evidently, by the late 1950s Italian couturiers were already having many of their designs produced industrially both in the US and Italy.

The next significant development took place in October 1960, when *WWD* reported widespread tie-ins between Italian couturiers and Italian ready-to-wear manufacturers. Avolio had designed a collection for Milanese manufacturer Abital, Marucelli for Alexandra of Ancona, and likewise, Galitzine and Biki for Cori (GFT), of Turin, Veneziani for Conber of Vicenza, Fabiani for Luigi Giannini of Turin, and Schuberth for Stylbert of Arezzo. *WWD* noted that 'Boutique has arrived in Italy in a big way.' It seems that by the start of the 1960s, Italian ready-to-wear was able to produce high-quality products for a specific section of the American mass-market. At the same time, it was becoming increasingly obvious that as the lifestyles of the international rich relaxed, the future of haute couture was becoming uncertain, but that the market for ready-to-wear was increasingly strong. Specifically, the fact that there was a growing international market for high-quality ready-to-wear, for which Italian production was well suited, was recognised in the industry, both in Italy and the US.

It is especially significant that in October 1960, 'just back from a visit to the US', Pucci told *WWD* that 'the future of high fashion belongs to the ready-to-wear industry. Today the couturier must figure out how to make the little suit or coat that will sell commercially at a high profit because of the label, in order to pay for the cost of making all the expensive dresses. As the ready-to-wear industry becomes more organised and more substantially equipped, it can achieve a lot that high fashion once did.' This comment indicates that profits from Italian couture may already have been meagre, as was clearly the case in the French couture industry.[30] As in Paris (where the drop in sales of haute couture after the War was already necessitating a reorganisation within this specific sector), the link between high fashion and ready-to-wear enabled Italian designers to meet the changing needs of the international market. This link also gave Italian manufacturers the necessary kudos to target the quality ready-to-wear market, as *WWD* wrote in March 1962: 'Couture names which add enough prestige to warrant the US retail price tag make commercial successes of Fabiani ready-to-wear, Simonetta Boutique, Veneziani Universale, De Barentzen's Bazaar, Fontana Export, Baratta Sport, Enzo's selections and Antonelli's ready-to-wear line, which in less than a year of existence has had to double its equipment in order to increase its output from the present 150 pieces a day. This situation applies mainly to the US market.'

The Significance of Knitwear in the Move Towards Volume Production The Italian knitwear industry boomed in the period under study. Indeed, it played an increasingly important part in the expansion of Italian ready-to-wear after the War, and it is vital to consider the significance of its early evolution as part of the wide expansion in export trade and the move towards serial production. The recollections of Florentine buyer Enzo Tayar provide an valuable insight into this specific development. Tayar explains that the international market for Italian fashion knitwear emerged soon after the War partly as a facet of the interest in elite Italian fashion, but also from the US craft-buying tradition, which Florentine buying offices had catered for since the early twentieth century. This was because at first Italian knitwear exports were almost entirely hand-produced at artisan level and can be seen as virtually couture.

According to Tayar, Italian knit was especially sought-after by the US in the post-war years 'because it was very different from anything made in America'. Although it is not yet known how far this factor was responsible for the extent of US demand, it seems likely that both the cheapness of the Italian product and the flexibility of the Italian producers to design and expand to US requirements, played a vital part in this growth. Tayar says that by the early 1950s there was 'a tremendous volume of exports and Americans spent millions of dollars every year on Italian knit, produced predominantly in the Carpi area, near Modena'. There was a bonanza for several years, especially after 1954, when the US stores began importing silk knits in large quantities. The market was approximately 50 per cent department store and speciality shop trade, and 50 per cent wholesale'. This is corroborated by *WWD* reports, which as early as February 1956, for example, ran the headline 'Italian knitwear producers expect exports to hit new high'. This was claimed on the basis of 'a spectacular increase' in official export figures from the Central Institute of Statistics, which jumped, in silk knits, for example, from $16,000 in 1954 to $40,000 in 1955. Silks formed the smallest export sector in Italian knit exports, but was the fastest growing. Wool and cotton rose from $4.5 million to $8 million in the same period. The boom continued in the early 1960s, and in April 1963, for example, one US 'sportswear merchandiser', Bill Hass, bought more than 52,000 mohair sweaters (retail $10–16) on one buying trip.

The most famous name in the Italian knitwear boom was 'Mirsa', a boutique level label run by the Marquesa di Gresy, who was credited in the same edition of *WWD* with 'making Italian knitwear a complete look' with her flat-knit two- and three-piece suits. Other internationally known names include Avagolf and Celli. The Missoni label, now internationally renowned for imaginatively coloured knitwear, was introduced in 1958, but the Missoni workshop and factory were not established until 1968, at Sumirago. Mirsa's strongest market was in the US, and probably her single biggest customer was Saks 5th Avenue, which sold large quantities of her designs. However, the international market for Italian knitwear ranged from high fashion names, such as Mirsa, to mass-market level. Indeed, one of the first US knitwear buyers to arrive in Italy was a representative of the US mass-market chain store 'Alexander's', as early as 1947. Alexander's signed an order with George Farkas of Carpi, a women's sweater producer, for one-piece dresses, in fine machine-knit wool, which for the Americans were very cheap. Tayar succinctly summarises the move towards industrialisation thus: 'at first the US department stores clamoured for individual hand-knits, and were happy to pay the prices asked by the Italian producers. As Italian knits became highly fashionable internationally, the stores demanded increased output, and began to look for machine-knits which could be more swiftly delivered. Simultaneously, US wholesalers picked up on the trend and pushed output even higher.'[31]

As sales increased, so the Italians expanded their knitwear production, establishing central 'factories' and moving into machine-production. These were of varying size. Many were small-scale, but by the late 1950s, Mirsa, for example had a 'big, modern factory', according to Enzo Tayar. *WWD* provides an explicit example of this, as early as June 1950, stating that 'for 20 years, Mrs Lea Galliani had been working for the dressmakers, boutiques and smart shops of Milan, creating high-style handmade sweaters. Two years ago she started creating machine-made sweaters too, and at present manages 50 per cent machine-work. Italian interests anticipate that Italy's ready-to-wear system will expand.' This was clearly of great interest to *WWD*'s trade readership. Tayar explains the move towards mechanisation thus: 'gradually the buyers were looking for better and better value for money, and so the Italian wholesalers started to compromise on quality, in favour of quantity, using bigger and bigger needles, for example. Once the US market developed, the European market piggybacked on it, and expanded slowly but surely.' US trade press coverage of Italian knitwear corroborates Tayar's statement. *WWD* covered knitwear regularly through the 1950s and 1960s, and in January 1957, for example, recorded that 'because of the needs of American buyers, Italian knitwear manufacturers are moving up their seasons so they can meet delivery dates'. Conversely, there is scant reference to the European export market, although this increases towards the end of the 1950s.

This is clear evidence that in knitwear, as in general high fashion apparel, Italy was guided towards serial production by the US market. Further, Tayar's testimony suggests that Italian knitwear was being produced at volume levels solely to meet US market demand, very soon after the Second World War, well before Italian high fashion sold to the US in any significant quantity. This indicates that the Italian move towards serial production for the export market was led at least in part, by knitwear and by the US response.

US Involvement in the Move Towards Mass-Market Italian Ready-to-Wear Production   It is widely accepted by historians and witnesses that there was no fashionable mass-market women's ready-to-wear production in Italy until well into the post-war period, at the level below boutique. However, Fairchild's coverage reveals that this may not in fact be true, through coverage of two key developments in this area of production, in the summer of 1960. Significantly, the US ready-to-wear industry was involved in both these episodes. The first concerned multi-branched middle market Italian department store La Rinascente, which had branches all over Italy, and its subsidiary Apem, which as *WWD* reported in April 1960, manufactured a wide range of ready-to-wear for Rinascente and other retailers, at an equivalent of $1.60–$300 wholesale. In May that year, *WWD* revealed that Apem was planning to launch an export programme and 'preliminary contacts with US and Canadian stores are reported as "thrilling"'. The report stated that 'according to Apem's executive director, the stores are not particularly interested in inexpensive garments, but in those that offer something different. Apem plans to carry into mass production designs by Galitzine, Capucci, Fabiani and Simonetta.'

In June, a licence contract between middle-market La Rinascente, and the US ready-to-wear manufacturer Donnybrook Fashions was announced, under the title 'Donnybrook Licences Coat Styles for Italian firm.' The deal was for the production of approximately 2,000 coats per week by Rinascente, to a minimum of twelve Donnybrook designs. The coats would be sold in Rinascente stores, and other outlets in Europe and America, whilst labels, advertising and promotion were under Donnybrook control. This meant cheap production for the Americans, as well as command of the marketing process. Fairchild claimed that the agreement would 'provide the Italian industry with a much needed boost'. It also signified an important step in relations between the US ready-to-wear industry and Italian manufacturing in the move towards volume production. The second development came less than a month later in July 1960, when *WWD* announced that US dress manufacturer Henry Rosenfeld had also signed a deal with La Rinascente for production of their designs, to be sold in Europe. This deal also included an agreement by Rosenfeld to purchase all their Italian fabrics through La Rinascente. The terms must have been mutually beneficial, because two years later in 1962, the contract was renewed.

Further moves towards increasing Italo-US trade and the consequential stimulation of Italian mass-production was already evident throughout the 1950s. In May 1952, Gordon Selfridge stressed to WWD that 'Italian manu-facturers should make an effort to standardise production, while limiting variety of output to goods currently in demand. In doing so, the Italian manufacturers would be able to reduce prices, especially as Italian labour costs are lower than in the US.' In the same article the Italian-American Marketing Council proposed new and detailed market research surveys on Italian exports to the US, 'with a view to increasing them', so that traditional exports would be 'substituted for more suitable goods required in the US'. In October that year, *WWD* reported a new Italian law was introduced to supply 'state insurance on all Italian exports and the elimination of the necessary export licenses on a wide range of goods to the dollar areas'. This implies that both US and Italian trade interests sought not only industrial expansion, but expansion in a specific direction to meet the particular needs of the US market.

However, perhaps the most significant evidence of industrial links between the US and Italian fashion industries is found in WWD in June 1958: 'The GFT will show for the first time a complete range of women's apparel. It is thought that this spring-summer collection will permit GFT to enter the American market.' Gruppo Finanzario Tessile was a Turin-based mass-market ready-to-wear manufacturer, which already successfully produced menswear. It was to become one of the most important Italian women's fashion and textile companies of the 1960s, and was to become one of the most profitable international fashion and textile firms of the twentieth century, with a central role in the celebrated international success of 'Italian style' from the 1970s. Since this first GFT women's ready-to-wear collection was specifically aimed at the US market, this report is solid confirmation that it was led into the mass-market by American sales. Although the collection was slow to take off in the European market, it was an important pointer towards the future relationship between GFT and high fashion designers, which was to become central to the group's success in later years.[32]

These were not isolated cases. In November 1959, WWD declared that 'resident buyers believe Italian ready-to-wear is catching on in the US and they are urging Italian manufacturers to take advantage of obvious American interest'. This article is particularly noteworthy because it contains a rare summary of the state of Italian ready-to-wear in that period. 'This is a field that was practically non-existent as far as American stores were concerned two or three years ago. Store representatives say Italian manufacturers still have much to learn about the American market, especially in sizing.' It was said that the Italian ready-to-wear industry consisted of about 100 factories, but that such mass-production was 'only part of a sprawling industry that takes in hundreds of small plants and thousands of cottage workers. The leading plants employ between 6–7,000 workers.' The report continued to say that ' accurate production figures are virtually non-existent. The 100 organised factories produce an estimated 1.25 million coats, suits and dresses annually. Apparel export figures to the US are not broken down to ready-to-wear, but it is believed that over half of all ready-to-wear shipped abroad goes to the US.'

Another *WWD* report in October the following year reiterated concerns with sizing, saying 'success or failure of the [1960 New York] presentation may well depend upon manufacturers providing proper sizings for American stores. Resident buyers in Florence, who are anxious for the Italian market to make a good first impression, have been repeatedly warning manufacturers that their sizes must be correct. All manufacturers who will be shown here have acquired American-sized mannequins and have been working out their models on them. A clause in all contracts written at showings will provide for cancellation of orders if sizing is incorrect.' Thus it is evident that by the end of the 1950s, the US trade was already very interested in mass-level Italian ready-to-wear, but clearly saw it as backward and underdeveloped, and was very keen for the industry to update itself to meet its particular needs, as soon as possible, because the US fashion trade saw Italy as a useful, competitively priced source for new products. This reading is supported by another revealing article, published in May 1960, in which concern was voiced that 'at present, European manufacturers just do not have the technique at which our own ready-to-wear producers are so skilled. It takes two or three times as long to put over an idea to a European plant as it does at home.'

More detailed information concerning the US sale of Italian mass-market ready-to-wear, can be gleaned from an October 1960 *WWD* review of the first collective presentation of Italian ready-to-wear in New York. Buyer attendance was organised by Enzo Tayar and his brother. Each manufacturer paid an entrance fee of around $800, and paid the organisers 2 per cent commission on all business done in the six-month season. Together with the cost of the trip, this represented a considerable outlay, so the sales prospects must have been promising. The participants included Abital of Milan, Alexandra of Ancona, Cori (GFT) of Turin, Conber of Vicenza, Luigi Giannini of Turin, Merving of Turin, Alma of Milan, Rosier of Milan, and Stylbert of Arezzo. This group was described as 'a fairly good cross-section of Italian ready-to-wear, ranging from products suitable for popular-priced department stores to better merchandise for quality speciality shops'. In fact, it was a good cross-section of high-quality ready-to-wear, with a number of the lines designed by couturiers. The audience included a wide range of American stores such as Bergdorf Goodman, Marshall Field, Bendel, Alexander and Ohrbach, as well as three Canadian stores. However, it is particularly significant because it shows that a high proportion of top Italian ready-to-wear firms were attempting to enter the US market as early as 1960, which is much earlier than any published sources have previously acknowledged.

Nonetheless, this journey was not entirely smooth. The *WWD* report registered complaints about high prices, remarking that most of the lines fell 'into the range which will retail between $40 to 65 in the US. Regular buyers for popular priced US stores, however, feel that if a real volume trade is to result, a retail price level below $30 will have to be found.' A few weeks later in November 1960 a *WWD* report entitled 'Italian ready-mades disappointing US buyers', criticised low market levels, remarking that 'retailers do not have to come to Italy for cotton dresses $9 or $10 first cost'. However, they judged Conber-Veneziani silk suits at $135 retail to be very saleable, and said that the line with 'the greatest commercial potential is that of Cori', whilst Apem was described as 'another line buyers feel is worth watching'. Significantly, the report added that 'the Italian ready-to-wear industry has much to learn'.

Crucially, however, such criticisms did nothing to curb American enthusiasm for Italian fashion, and the spring 1961 couture/boutique collections in Florence enjoyed a record attendance, which indicates that *WWD*'s comments were intended to mould Italian production to their requirements, rather than to discourage it. In January of that year *WWD*, reported that 'Buyer attendance here numbers reps from 219 retail and manufacturing organisations . . . 26 more than last year, and the first time it has topped the 200 mark.' This included a number of US ready-to-wear manufacturers, such as Anita Modes, F Haar Originals, Kimberley Knitwear, Joseph Love Dresses, Daniel Millstein Inc., Suzy Perette, Hannah Troy, Zelinka Matlick, and Ben Zuckerman. This is further evidence that US trade interests were keen to push Italian manufacturers further towards volume production, but in precise directions. Clearly, they did not simply want what the US ready-to-wear industry already produced so efficiently – cheap mass-produced reasonably stylish clothes. Rather, they wanted value-for-money, quality and quantity. This did not mean the lowest levels of manufacture, but specific mass-produced middle and upper ranges of seasonally stylish ready-to-wear.

This area of Italian specialisation was certainly recognised by the early 1960s. In March 1962 Marjorie Harlepp stated (erroneously) in *WWD* that 'Italian ready-to-wear has not reached, and probably never will achieve, the mass-production volume achieved by the US or even Germany.' However, she continued: 'That type of operation is not the Italian forte, which is small, original, exclusive fashions with plenty of variety.' The report conceded, however, that by this stage, 'mass-production is achieved, mostly in sportswear, ranging from the confections of Pucci to the bread and butter works of Apem, and Famatex of Milan, Roslein and Panfin of Florence, Saba of Alessandria, and a handful of Prato manufacturers, who make shirts and slacks of low-priced or reprocessed woollens. These goods are sold to so many US and Canadian stores and chains that it is impossible to list them, and in quantities which appear in the official export figures as follows: for 11 months – $8 mill in 60, 9.5 mill in 1961.'

Italians manufacturers remained keen to respond positively to US analysis, and as *WWD* reported in May 1961, Giorgini announced that he was 'confident that manufacturers have learned from the mistakes of the first show held last November, and will produce lines of interest to the US'. At this show, middle market lines Apem and Cori 'were outstanding both for prices and styling, stressing a relaxed and casual look'. As a result, exports rose even more quickly at this point. According to *WWD* in October 1961, in the first half of 1961 alone, apparel exports increased by 35 per cent, compared to the first half of 1960. In 1950, world-wide exports of Italian 'sewn goods' were $5 million; 'the proportion is equally striking when referred to the US; from nearly $600,000 in 1950, Italian apparel exports have reached $10,322,000 at the end of 1961'. By 1961 the figures had risen to $83 million, *WWD* reported in March 1962. This made the US the single most important buyer of Italian apparel. In fact, at this point the US imported one-fifth of all Italian ready-to-wear and in turn, Italian apparel accounted for 16.2 per cent of overall American imports from Italy from 1960, an increase that exceeded that of the other six European importers.

These are extremely important instances of direct US involvement in Italian volume production at mass-market level in the early post-war period. They suggest that the US fashion trade deliberately set out to encourage Italian production in this direction. It is important however, to note that even in the early 1960s, Italy's vastly increased exports to the US only represented about 2 per cent of the total American consumer expenditure on clothing and accessories. According to Fairchild research department figures, reported in *WWD* in February 1960, 'Soaring imports' were 'still only a drop in the bucket', so it is not surprising that the US fashion industry continued to press for further increase, and that their manufacturers did not feel threatened by it. In March 1962, WWD explained this concisely, in a piece entitled 'Italy needs US technicians to lead the way from the cottage'. It declared that 'the apparel production in this country [Italy], is the result of about a thousand industrial or semi-industrial firms and several thousands of indefinable firms where an entrepreneur assigns and collects work done by cottage workers and small laboratories. At the same time, the annual apparel output's growth is estimated at 25–30 per cent, the highest in the Western countries.' The report concluded that 'this fast development is more a direct consequence of booming exports rather than of the rising domestic demand. However, every year, many more men and women buy ready made clothes (and will buy more when the retail trade improves its structure). Undoubtedly, the present trend toward apparel industrialisation derives from exports.'

In the early 1960s, finally, a further important development emerged in the Italian ready-to-wear industry, which was linked not to the US, but to the European market. Following the establishment of the Common Market in 1958, European trade liberalised, and the appearance in Italy of buyers from a number of other European countries increased considerably. By March 1962, *WWD* was able to reveal that the Turin apparel showmart SAMIA (established in 1955) had been visited by '1,000 non-American buyers' in the previous year. However, these buyers were not especially interested in quality Italian ready-to-wear, but bought 'at all levels', according to *WWD*. Such sales were increasingly important to the Italian fashion industry, and at the first national congress organised by the Apparel Manufacturers Association in Montecatini in October 1962, the possibilities offered by import-export trade in the Common Market and the US, was one of the main discussion topics. Significantly, this expansion of European trade was seen by contemporary commentators as the result of American groundwork, as *WWD* stated, 'the European market, especially with the Common Market, has absorbed "Made in Italy" clothes; business already done with American importers and retailers have been a helpful training'. As a consequence of booming interest, in June 1963, *WWD* published an official forecast for apparel production for the period up to 1970, of a 10 per cent increase in sales per annum.

It is clear that pressure from the US market to expand production was exerted predominantly on the high fashion levels of Italian fashion from the early to late 1950s, and that the possibilities of volume production were demonstrated to Italian high fashion designers through the reproduction of their creations by US retailers and manufacturers. Some boutique houses, such as Pucci, also began designing very high-quality ready to wear for the US market very soon after the War ended, and this was followed by movement into high fashion ready-to-wear by couture designers, encouraged all the while by US retailers and manufacturers.

What has been neglected by research to date is that at the same time, another group of Italian ready-to-wear manufacturers was emerging, in the middle-high quality market. Such companies as GFT cannot be classified as 'boutique', and did not participate in the collective showings in Florence, but this chapter has shown that a significant number of them responded eagerly to US pressure for expansion, and made their international sales debut in America, often at the very start of their ready-to-wear production in the late 1950s. This group of manufacturers was to become central to the post-war international success of Italian fashion. All the available evidence points, therefore, towards a significant US push for the development of volume sales of Italian garments, made to specific US sizing requirements, and at a specific, high-quality level.

The Use of US Production Techniques and Machinery in Italian Fashion

Although there was a menswear clothing industry in Italy before the Second World War, by the immediate post-war years ready-to-wear production was still organised 'like a large tailor's shop', and there was no established apparel machinery manufacturing industry in Italy.[33] Consequently, almost all machinery used in the embryonic ready-to-wear industry had to be imported. However, there were increasing opportunities for Italian entrepreneurs to learn about US manufacturing methods, machinery, and the US market through their dealings with the US fashion trade.

WWD journalist Elisa Massai confirms that some of the earliest post-war contact between the two industries came via Italian textiles' representatives travelling in the US in search of markets: 'this was one important way that Italian fashion producers learnt about US fashion, including industrial organisation, technology and machinery, as well as the market and its style'.[34] The initial impact came in terms of organisation. Massai remembers that both textile and fashion manufacturers who went to the US were extremely impressed with the efficiency and low cost of their industry, and were very keen to know how the US system operated.

As early as November 1949, *WWD* announced the forthcoming opening of the new Rinascente department store in Milan, and revealed that many US retailing ideas would be incorporated. The chairman had already made a trip to the US some months previously, and said that he and his technicians received much hospitality and excellent suggestions from numerous American department store executives. It was only a few months later that US ready-to-wear manufacturers Donnybrook and Rosenfeld made their production deals with Rinascente. It is particularly significant that the deals included the 'installation of American equipment and American key men'. These men were representatives of the American firms who had been selected to supervise production and train Italian workers in American production methods. In July 1950 *WWD* concluded that this was 'likely to develop Italy's ready-to-wear garment industry which has found since the War that the present artisan work on which the trade largely depends, is too costly and too slow. Italian interests anticipate that Italy's ready-to-wear system will expand.'

For their part, Rinascente accepted that they were well aware of the need to install mass production methods and said that they were purchasing machinery to fill these needs. Much of this involved the buying of modern cutting, pleating and stitching machines from the Ginsberg Machinery Company Inc. By September 1950, *DNR* reported that Maurice Shapiro of Ginsberg had arrived in Italy from the US to survey the re-equipment needs of La Rinascente's factory. Mr Shapiro made a recommendation for the purchase of machinery costing over $100,000. The plant started production in December 1950, with an output of 300 garments per week, but was not expected to be in full production until the spring. The products of the agreement were advertised in *Linea Italiana* in 1951, as 'Rosenfeld, New York models, at La Rinascente' as seen in figure 4. The advertisement promised that the garments, exemplified by a dress and a suit, resolved a problem which greatly interested most women, with their 'simple elegance, practicality, youth', as well as 'impeccable sizing, perfect execution, and modern colours and sizes' at reasonable prices.

The contract was evidently successful because it was renewed in 1952 and by 1960, the Rinascente Apem plant was producing 5,000 pieces daily, according to *WWD*, reporting in May 1960. At this point Apem was described as Italy's biggest women's apparel plant, covering 34,000 square feet, and had reached a daily output of 3,000 garments, with a figure of 5,000 predicted by the end of the year. It is certain that neither such high levels of production, nor the market lead, would have been possible without the early kick-start of US machinery and expertise.

Figure 4. Advertisement for La Rinascente/Rosenfeld ready-to-wear garments.
Source: *Linea Italiana*, Spring 1951, p. 34.

However, little further specific evidence of such deals has been traced in the 1950s, and it may be that Rinascente's case was not representative. Even by the early 1960s, Italy's technological development in this sphere was far from advanced, and it is interesting that only the manufacturers with the highest international profiles were seen to have modernised. In March 1962, Signor Moreschi, the secretary of the National Apparel Manufacturing Association, told *WWD* that 'Italy Needs US Technicians to Lead the Way from the Cottage'. *WWD* explained that the need for technicians and the traditional distribution system were the most serious obstacles to a co-ordinated expansion of the Italian ready-to-wear industry. The industry was said to be at a crucial point: 'while a few additional seamstresses may still be found in the great reserve of cottage, textile, and artisan workers, the manufacturing technician is almost absent. Up until now, the owner, helped by relatives, has managed to establish a nucleus of industrial organisation. A few Milan and Turin manufacturers (Facis, Sidinec, Cori, Apem, Marzotto, Rosier etc) decided to have the most up-to-date factories and hired technicians from the US, Germany and Switzerland. The great majority, however, of the Italian firms are far from knowing what modern production means.'

One of the greatest obstacles identified by Moreschi was the lack of training available in Italy concerning modern garment production systems. He stressed that there were no schools, except for some courses organised inside some factories, 'suited to prepare apparel manufacturing technicians: a hundred women's professional schools maintain the tradition of skilled hand-labour, which should be tuned to more modern production systems'. The Association, according to Moreschi, was planning a specialised institute for the preparation of apparel technicians and executives. The project required a lot of money, partly from the Italian government, but it was said that 'the big, serious problem is finding instructors'.

At this point, the US was still seen as the most important source of technology and technological personnel, in the quest for modernisation. This is further endorsed by a report published by Fairchild in 'Electronics News', in November 1960 which suggested that 'Present machine tool production by Italian firms, covers only half what is needed in this country, although substantial expansion has taken place in the last decade. Italian industrialists are ready to spend their money in modernising and perfecting their plants, accepting everything good and suitable made in America or Europe.'

There are also many examples of both the ad hoc method of gleaning technological information from the US and the use of US machinery. The direct use of imported US machinery is the most difficult to trace. Although it is certain that Marzotto's first women's ready-to-wear collections were produced at a new factory 'equipped with American machinery' in 1963 (*WWD* October 1963), it is not clear what type of machines were installed and no other references have been found in Fairchild's reports. Fortunately, there is more detailed evidence concerning the use of industrial organisation. References in *WWD* are fairly regular, but tend to be brief. In November 1961, for example, the journal reported that Italian representative Signor Ceccarini was leaving for a month's visit to the US: 'Mr Ceccarini will spend most of his time in New York, he will also visit the various Burlington plants, for a refresher study on techniques and products.' Both MaxMara and GFT had strong links with the US fashion industry in different ways and offer useful case studies.

MaxMara has not kept detailed records of its early development, but its founder Achille Maramotti has explained his dealings with the US in interview.[35] MaxMara did not sell to American markets in this period, yet Maramotti was very well aware of technological developments on that side of the Atlantic. Although German technology in this field was advanced when compared to Italian production, Maramotti stresses that Italian manufacturers always tried to build up more contact with the US than with Germany in these years. This was partly because US technology and concepts were extremely advanced, and partly because the US product image was closer to the Italian one (or at least, the one that Maramotti sought). Maramotti stresses additionally the importance of the foremen working in the US clothing factories, many of whom were of Italian origin and who were easily persuaded to discuss new garment-making processes. Many of the owners, buyers and distributors in the US garment trade were also of Italian origin and were also interested in helping the fledgling Italian industry to find its feet.

MaxMara's first coat, produced in 1951, was unfitted, and this was crucial because it would accommodate almost anyone. Apart from the traditional snobbery attached to women wearing only individual made-to-measure clothes, in Italy, ready-to-wear was still considered to be of very poor quality and ill-fitting. Maramotti bypassed this latter stumbling-block, at least with this coat. The first suit presented more of a problem. Fashionable suits, which followed the 'New Look' launched by Paris couturier, Dior, in 1947, were extremely fitted and intricately constructed. The mass-production of such complex cut and fit was a considerable challenge. It presented far more difficulties, than, for example, a 1920s sheath dress, which was the type of garment that many British and American ready-to-wear companies cut their teeth on. Maramotti's solution was to produce a suit fully lined with 'pello di camelo', a strong canvas fabric, so that the outfit was firm, with its own shape and cut in the usual range of sizes, would appear to fit all customers far better than it actually did. This suit formed the other half of the first MaxMara 'collection', in winter 1951. There were then, as we have seen, still no ready-to-wear outlets in Italy, so Maramotti convinced fabric retailers to put the designs in the corner of their stores to see if they would sell. They did, and the range sold out.

MaxMara's American manufacturing contact was Picone, who ran a small made-to-measure tailoring company, and who had emigrated from Sicily to New York in 1936. Soon after his arrival he had co-founded the women's ready-to-wear label 'Evan Picone'. In the mid-1950s, Maramotti visited him in America and was very interested by his manufacturing methods. He saw how they made coats and suits and followed their example. Maramotti insists that the major technological concepts which shaped Italian ready-to-wear came from the United States. He cites, for example, multi-layer cutting techniques, as well as the vital notion of the production line; for Maramotti, the most crucial influence came from the concept of 'efficient industrial organisation'. However, the idea of hanging garments on a conveyor which travels between processes, minimising handling, was Maramotti's own, he says. The machinery came initially from both the US and Germany (button-hole machines, for example, were American made), but once it was produced domestically, it made sense to patronise domestic machine engineering suppliers. He is proud of the fact that between 1950 and 1965 the man hours required to make a MaxMara coat decreased from 18 to just 2 hours, yet quality was maintained.

Unfortunately, there are no surviving members of the Rivetti family who experienced GFT's early post-war development, but a proportion of the group's extensive records are preserved in the company archive at Turin and a 'notebook' entitled *Appunti sull'evoluzione del Gruppo GFT: Un'analisi condotta sui fondi_dell'Archivio storico* has been published to accompany its recent reorganisation.[36] Although partial and incomplete, this notebook attempts to trace the different stages of GFT's growth through the surviving documentation available and offers an important insight into the industrial organisation and mechanisation of the group in the post-war period. GFT was formed in 1930 from the merger of two Italian companies, owned by the Levi and Rivetti families. In the 1860s, David Levi had started trading in textiles around Turin, whilst Giuseppe Rivetti had set up a textile mill near Biella. In 1932 they moved into men's ready-made clothing, known as 'confezione', with the label 'Facis'. By the outbreak of the Second World War, Facis was the 'largest and oldest manufacturer of men's and boy's garments', and was especially well-known for suits.[37]

However, according to the notebook, production was still organised like a large tailor's shop and it was not until the 1950s that GFT began a radical structural reorganisation programme. This programme was undertaken because it was clear to the new Rivetti generation that 'a great season was approaching for the ready-to-wear manufacturer, and it was necessary to be ready'. This understanding of the changing apparel market came directly from their experiences in the US. The notebook explains that the Rivettis 'had studied and travelled extensively, and expected the Western consumption model, centred on the US's example, to spread around the world and to become the dominant trend'. They thus expected new types of demand and consumption in Italy, and responded accordingly with the introduction of mass production. Luigi Settembrini, who was a PR consultant for GFT in the 1960s, recalls that the three Rivetti brothers, Piergiorgio, Franco, and Silvio, had in fact travelled to the US in the very early 1950s, specifically in order to understand the American production system.[38] Indeed he says that links with US industry had been established in the inter-war period by the owner of Levi, who had travelled there, although probably for marketing purposes. Until 1954 the group still included the Biella textile mills, but since Biella entrepreneurs were resistant to mass production, the brothers sold their shares in the mills and took complete control of GFT, which was the only unit equipped to face the new demands of mass production.

The role of the US in the transformation of the GFT group did not end with an understanding of changing markets, and the need to industrialise. US manufacturing techniques were directly imported, with the assistance of Italian-American experts. The GFT of 1954 was not yet equipped to attempt standardisation of its products. It was necessary, therefore, to concentrate on the production process, 'in order to fit mass production techniques imported from the US to the Italian situation'.[39] The notebook specifies that it was Silvio Rivetti, in particular, who prompted the innovation, and who 'took advantage of the co-operation of Italian-American experts'. These experts are identified as Italian 'immigrant tailors, who had built up their own experience during the growth of the American clothing industry'. Unfortunately, no names are given, but it is important to note that this group of immigrants also included, for example, Evan Picone, MaxMara's US contact.

The desire for manufacturing innovation, and the advice of these 'experts' led to the famous decision to make what is known in the firm as 'the sizing revolution', and what Maramotti refers to as a seminal 'anthropometric survey'. GFT sought to improve their range of sizes, and in 1954 asked salesmen and shopkeepers to record the measurements of their customers, measuring a sample of 25,000, to produce the *Sistema 120 Taglia* (120 sizes) for ready-made suits, in 1958. This was the first time in Italy that ready-to-wear sizing had reproduced actual physiognomic features, rather than standard abstract sizes. According to Luigi Settembrini, 'the idea came from America'. Further innovations were made in field of marketing, including the introduction of recommended retail prices, a new logo, and reorganised distribution, and by the mid-1950s, a large new factory had been opened in Settimo, near Turin, although the origins of the machinery used are not known.

The 'Cori' women's ready-to-wear line was introduced by GFT in 1958. It is described as 'extremely diversified, and very flexible, ranging over age groups, shapes and quality levels', and by the early 1960s included several trademarks, such as Cori Lady (outsize), Cori Junior (teenage), and Cori Biki (upmarket).[40] Once again, the liaison between Italian couture and ready-to-wear became evident. Cori had begun working with the Italian couturier Biki in 1958, and a formal agreement was signed in 1961. The deal involved the design of a certain number of 'exclusive' models for Cori, and Biki's presence at various promotional events.

GFT's links with the US continued into the 1960s. Settembrini recalls, for example, that one of the Rivettis returned from the US in the early 1960s with the idea of 'Wash'n'Wear' jackets. At the Rome Olympics in 1960, GFT introduced the 'Madras' men's jacket, which could be sat on without wrinkling, and which was very useful for wearing to the games. This garment, Settembrini says, came directly from the US, even in its styling. It can be seen therefore that GFT's approach to ready-to-wear production, and in particular the understanding of and response to the market, came from learnt experience in the US. As another GFT notebook puts it, 'Italian industry . . . found itself forced to shift from its pre-industrial dimensions to industrialisation in the best 'American' style . . . in the direction of the mass market'.[41]

In Italian knitwear production, the relationship with the US fashion industry is more ambiguous and it is more difficult to pinpoint whether modernisation was led by Italian producers, or ultimately by the US market. The industrial structure and mechanisation of the knitwear production has been usefully described in some detail by the buyer Enzo Tayar. Tayar makes the important point that 'US ready-to-wear factories were the example followed in the immediate post-war years, when Italy had no industry to speak of. The American ideas were interpreted strictly, especially in terms of cutting corners, and coming up with a good product at a low price.' As in mainstream apparel, sizing in Italian knitwear came from the US. In 1951 American dressmakers' dummies, in standard sizes, were sent to the Italian producers, 'because they could not possibly operate on the old system'. Again, Tayar stresses the importance of the industrial links with Italo-Americans in the US fashion industry, although he cannot remember dealing with any Italo-American buyers. In conclusion, he states that the Italian producers had to adapt their methods to the American market in order to get the business and states that 'this was the key to Italian success'.[42]

Higher up the fashion ladder, Pucci's production offers a different example of expanding production, and one which was also strongly linked to demand in the US market, as we have seen. His changing production methods clearly indicate an acceptance of the need to meet changing markets and expand sales internationally. This process has been described in detail by Carla Strini. At first, the collections were made at Pucci's ancestral palace in Florence. Here he sketched his ideas, and these were interpreted into garments by a 'maestra' called Signora Ida, who had twelve girls working under her direction by the early 1950s. In the early stages of Pucci's fashion career, all the fittings were done on the body in the couture tradition and the grading methods were unconventional and unstandardised, developed ad hoc by Signora Ida and Pucci. For example, the fit of the crotch was measured by sitting the model on a table and measuring from the waist to the top of the table. However, by the time Strini joined in 1954, most garments were assembled outside the palace, mainly by homeworkers, using both German (Pfaff) and American (Singer) sewing machines. The 'important' items were still cut by hand, sewn and fitted at the palace.[43]

However, from 1956 the famous ready-to-wear shirts began to be made at Florence shirt factory 'Maggi', to Pucci's patterns. This important move towards standardisation and mass-production was made, according to Strini, for three highly significant reasons. Firstly, because 'by this time demand from America was so great', secondly because the shirts were 'such a simple cut', and could be easily reproduced by machine, and thirdly because 'Pucci felt that the quality and sizing would be more dependable if they were produced industrially'. Dependable quality and sizing are recurrent themes in the US trade press coverage in these years, and it seems highly likely that all these three points relate to US demand. Although Pucci's production was still on a 'small industrial basis' when compared to contemporary American models, his operations expanded considerably during Strini's employment there, and by the mid-late 1950s, significantly, they were beginning to sell in volume internationally. Strini dates Pucci's major expansion from 1958, and the 'industrial organisation' of the business to the early 1960s. This represents a large step away from the small-scale Italian high fashion production of the early 1950s.

Further evidence of the stimulation of Italian mass production by the US fashion industry can be seen in the Fontana factory, also at the highest ready-to-wear level. Although Micol Fontana resists referring to it as 'ready-to-wear', and insists that hand-finishing was important from the start in 1959, the plant was fully mechanised from its inception in 1959 and employed 400 people. Whilst they used Italian machinery by Necchi (because by the 1960s, according to Fontana, this company was producing all the factory equipment they needed), it is highly significant that Fontana says that 'the factory was run on American production models, with technology taken from America. Everybody did the same.'[44]

Conclusion

By 1965, Italian fashion production had expanded on all levels at an unprecedented rate. In that year *WWD*, predicted that 'industrially produced garments should reach a 70 per cent level, as against 30 per cent from artisan sources, thanks to the fast expanding demand for women's ready-to-wear styles'. Italy was also exporting at unprecedented levels, from haute couture to quality ready-to-wear. However, it was still more successful internationally at high fashion than at mass-production, and could not be considered fully automated until the early 1970s.

Nonetheless, by 1965 a group of major Italian ready-to-wear manufacturers were firmly established, who had set up modern factories and were producing fashionable, high-quality garments. The majority of these were reaching international markets, and many began their export drive in the US. Moreover, US expertise and technology was absolutely fundamental to the expansion of these manufacturers. Although the significance of the use of American machinery remains uncertain, it is clear that in certain cases it was crucial to expansion, and that in others, it was not. Also fundamental were the use of US contacts, the employment of US personnel, and the gleaning of production techniques from dealings with US retailers and manufacturers in the 1949–60 period.

Notes

1. Settembrini, Luigi, 'From Haute Couture to Prêt-à-Porter', in Celant, Germano, (ed.), *Italian Metamorphosis 1943–68*, Guggenheim, New York, 1994, p. 485.

2. For further details see Butazzi, Grazietta, *1922–1943 Vent'Anni di Moda Italiana*, Centro Di, Florence, 1980.

3. Brown silk two-piece gown, made in Tuscany, 1881. Label reads 'G. Giabbani/Sarta'. Pitti Palace, TA 1913, n.1806.

4. For further information see the catalogue to the Salvatore Ferragamo Museum in Florence, Ricci, Stephania (ed.), *Salvatore Ferragamo: the Art of the Shoe*, Mondadori, Milan, 1995.

5. Butazzi, Grazietta, *1922–1943 Vent'Anni di Moda Italiana*, Centro Di, Florence, 1980.

6. Enzo Tayar in interview, Florence, 18.10.95.

7. Di Castro, Federica, 'Italian High Fashion', in Butazzi, Grazietta et al., *Italian Fashion, Volume 1: The Origins of High Fashion and Knitwear*, Electa, Milan, 1987, p. 212.

8. Carter, Ernestine, *With Tongue in Chic*, Michael Joseph, London, 1974, p. 133.

9. These figures do not include private and gift buying. At the same date, the merchandise total of sewn goods was just over that of textiles, at $4,764,618, against $4,138,588.

10. For further details, see Lee Levin, Phyliss, *The Wheels of Fashion*, Doubleday, New York, 1965 and Kidwell, Claudia B. and Christman, Margaret C., *Suiting Everyone: the Democratisation of Clothing in America*, Smithsonian Institute, Washington D.C., 1974.

11. Both Kidwell and Christman, in *Suiting Everyone: the Democratisation of Clothing in America*, ibid., p. 63, and Sarah Levitt, in *Victorians Unbuttoned*, Allen

and Unwin, London, 1986, p. 77 and in *The Textile Society Journal*, 9, Spring 1988, pp. 2–13, 'Clothing Production and the Sewing Machine', pinpoint the machine-production of complete women's ready-to-wear outfits from the 1860s, in America and Britain respectively, following the first mass-production of the sewing machine in America from 1851. The current system of '8,10,12' was established in America during the First World War. This system markedly improved the fit of ready-to-wear, and spread worldwide from there.

12. *Home Life in America*, 1910, quoted in *Suiting Everyone: the Democratisation of Clothing in America*, ibid., p. 143.

13. Nelli, Humbert, *From Immigrants to Ethnics: the Italian-Americans*, Oxford University Press, Oxford, 1983, pp. 159–60. See also Handlin, Oscar, 'The Sweating System in New York', in *Immigration as a Factor in American History*, Prentice Hall, New Jersey, 1959, p. 64.

14. Nystrom, Paul, *The Economics of Fashion*, Ronald Press, New York, 1928, p. 481.

15. Film of a Giorgini interview, reproduced in 'La Sala Bianca: the Birth of Italian Fashion', (video), VideoCast, Florence, 1992.

16. Ghini interview, Florence, 17.10.95.

17. Film of a Giorgini interview, reproduced in 'La Sala Bianca: the Birth of Italian Fashion', (video), VideoCast, Florence, 1992.

18. Massai interview, Milan, 19.7.95.

19. Massai archive statistics, taken directly from the Italian Central Institute of Statistics.

20. See for example, Aragno, Bonizza Giordani, 'Project and Industry', in Bianchino, Gloria, *Italian Fashion Designing 1945–1980*, CSAC University of Parma, 1987, p. 45.

21. Ghini recalled in interview (Florence, 17.10.95), for example, that although British store buyers did attend, 'there were not very many of them, and they were not very important'. They included Swan and Edgar, Peter Jones and Woolands.

22. Ghini interview, Florence, 17.10.95.

23. Ibid. This is verified by Maria Pezzi, Micol Fontana and Carla Strini (in interview), who all attended the shows.

24. Ibid.

25. See for example, Kennedy, Shirley, *Pucci, a Renaissance in Fashion*, Abbeville, New York, 1991 and le Bourhis, Katell, Ricci, Stefania and Settimbrini, Luigi, *Emilio Pucci: Looking at Fashion*, Skira, Florence, 1996.

26. Example taken from the F.I.T. Costume Collection, New York.

27. Kennedy, Shirley, *Pucci: a Renaissance in Fashion*, Abbeville, New York, 1991, p. 113.

28. Butazzi, Grazietta, in the introduction to *Italian Fashion: Volume 1: The Origins of High Fashion and Knitwear*, Electa, Milan, 1987, p. 8.

29. Fontana (interview 23.10.95.) cannot remember the names of the manufacturers, 'because there were so many', but specifies that the royalties received under the licences were between 5–10 per cent.

30. The relationship between Paris couture and the ready-to-wear industry was addressed by the author in an unpublished BA (Hons) thesis entitled 'The Commercialisation of the Paris Haute Couture Industry 1947–65', University of Brighton, 1986.

31. Tayar interview, Florence, 18.10.95.

32. For further details, see Berta, Giuseppe (ed.), *Appunti sull'Evoluzione del Gruppo GFT: Un'Analisi Condotta sui fondi dell'Archivio Storico*, GFT, Turin, 1987, pp. 49–51.

33. Ibid., p. 15.

34. Massai interview, Milan, 19.7.95.

35. Maramotti interview, Reggio Emilia, 21.7.95.

36. In 1986 a major project was launched to organise the archives, and several 'notebooks' have been published on specific areas of the archive. See Berta, Giuseppe, (ed.), *Appunti sull'Evoluzione del Gruppo GFT: Un'Analisi Condotta sui Fondi dell'Archivio Storico*, GFT, Turin, 1987.

37. Abruzzo, Alberto, *Facis, Sidi, Cori: un' Analisi Condotta sui Ffondi dell'Archivio Storico sulla Grafica e la Pubblicita dal 1954 al 1979*, GFT, Turin, 1989, p. 22. The Facis trademark stood for 'factory produced suits', (Fabbrica Abiti Confezionati in Serie).

38. Luigi Settembrini in interview, Florence, 17.10.95. Settembrini was Public Relations consultant for GFT's ready-to-wear collections (Cori and Facis) from the early 1960s until the 1980s, when Cori was the women's wear line and Facis the men's. Until February 1996 he was Fashion and Communication consultant at the Italian fashion promotion organisation 'Pitti Immagine', and is currently Director of the Biennale di Firenze. Settembrini was also a Curator of the 1994 'Italian Metamorphosis' exhibition at the Guggenheim Museum, New York.

39. Berta, Giuseppe (ed.), *Appunti sull'Evoluzione del Gruppo GFT: Un'Analisi Condotta sui Fondi dell'Archivio Storico*, GFT, Turin, 1987, p. 49.

40. Abruzzo, Alberto, *Facis, Sidi, Cori: un' Analisi Condotta sui Fondi dell'Archivio Storico sulla Grafica e la Pubblicita dal 1954 al 1979*, GFT, Turin, 1989, p. 26. At least one additional line was added each year. Other examples include Cori Tre in spring 1963 and Cori Holiday in autumn 1963.

41. Abruzzo, Alberto, *Facis, Sidi, Cori: un' Analisi Condotta sui Fondi dell'Archivio Storico sulla Grafica e la Pubblicita dal 1954 al 1979*, GFT, Turin, 1989, p. 58.

42. Tayar interview, Florence, 18.10.95.

43. Strini interview, near Florence, 18.10.95.

44. Fontana interview, Rome, 23.10.95.

3

The Development of Italian Fashion Style

Italian Style Before 1951

Well-off Italian women in the post-war period looked to Paris for their fashion and bought from Paris haute couturiers where possible, as their mothers and grandmothers had done. The subservience of Italian dressmakers to French stylistic lead, even from the 1880s, is manifest in surviving Italian garments and even garment labels, which might read, for example, 'Frederic Vinti: Modes et Coiffeurs'.[1] The alternative to French couture was the extensive network of Italian court and private dressmakers, many of whom had very good reputations, and achieved very high technical and aesthetic standards, especially with embroidery.

Despite their quality, it was normal practice for the top professional dressmakers to import designs from Paris, and copy or 'translate' them. By the inter-war years there were three principle agencies, known as 'Model Houses' (Modellisti) which facilitated this process: Rina Modelli, Villa and Trellini. Maria Pezzi, who began work for an agency from 1936, has a unique private archive of her own fashion drawings, and has described both this process and her role within it in interview.[2] One example of her drawn reworkings of Paris couture from the post-war years is seen in figure 5. Pezzi explains that these model houses employed illustrators to alter French designs for the Italian market as soon as they were seen at the Paris collections. The translations were made in two principal ways. Firstly, there was a concentration on additional or alternative decoration, which reflects the Italian tradition of great craftsmanship, and secondly, the original cut was usually simplified, in line with the so-called 'poorer' Italian market.[3] The 'translated' designs were then shown collectively by the model houses to the smarter Italian dressmakers, who purchased them in the form of toiles or patterns and then copied them for the Italian market. A toile is a cotton reproduction of the original model, bearing the crucial details of cut and finish, but sold at a substantially lower price. Exclusivity, together with the right to use the original Paris name could only be obtained at considerable extra cost.

Figure 5. Illustration of a black and red check suit by Maria Pezzi for Tiziano, Autumn/Winter 1949–50. Source: Pezzi archive, Milan. Courtesy of Maria Pezzi.

Reduction of the dependence of Italian dressmakers on Paris style was integral to the fascist pursuit of self-sufficiency in the 1923–43 period, and there was a determined government effort to establish 'La Linea Italiana' (Italian style) based on notions of regional peasant dress. In 1932 the Ente Nazionale della Moda Italiana (National Fashion Office) was established in Turin to consolidate top dressmakers and manufacturers in order to achieve these aims. All 'high fashion' dressmakers were compelled by law to make 25 per cent of their production to original designs, which bore the trademark *Ideazione e Produzione Nazionale* (Conceived and Made in Italy).[4] In return, from 1933 onwards designers were offered both financial and promotional government support, including official exhibitions of both Italian textiles and fashion. In 1941 *Bellezza* was established as the 'official magazine' of the Ente, and published many articles in support of an independent Italian style.

In September 1942, *Bellezza* published an article entitled 'Collections Prepared for Foreigners' which used Italian topography as a metaphor to describe the progress of Italian fashion. The text encapsulates the ambitions of the Mussolini regime: 'When you climb a mountain, you can look back and see how far you've come. Many people saw the path as un-climbable. They thought that real elegance could only reach the Italian woman from across the Alps (France) or across the ocean (the United States). Italy continued to use foreign models, to copy or adapt to Italian taste. To continue on this path would not have been useful to Italy's economy. The War put up barriers between Italy and those who considered themselves to be the centre of international fashion. These barriers acted like a green house and gave Italian fashion the strength to blossom.' It was claimed that Italy was by this stage producing 'refined and practical models which are perfectly in tune with the new rhythm of life. Italian fashion has achieved a prominent position in Europe, and will know in future how to use this position.'

This claim to national and international eminence was patently erroneous and exaggerated for propaganda purposes and it is now evident that the whole operation was fundamentally ineffective. Yet the references to refinement, practicality and modern life were important indicators of the future development of Italian style. It is clear that by the outbreak of war, there was no Italian fashion industry, nor an independently innovative 'Italian style' which was recognisable to the international market, peasant-inspired or otherwise. Nonetheless, fascist involvement represented an energising force in Italian fashion, because it demonstrated that it was possible to work without French stylistic leadership.

After the Second World War, as French style recaptured its reputation as the global centre of elegance, and despite the fact that although the Paris couture industry experienced difficulties when it reappeared immediately after the armistice, in 1947 the world's eyes were firmly re-focused on Paris when Christian Dior launched his 'New Look'. Dior's opulent style with its long full or pencil skirts, narrow waists and rounded shoulders formed a stark contrast to the box-jackets and short, straight skirts of wartime, and was eagerly accepted by the international fashion press and by fashion-conscious, better-off women in both Europe and America.[5] Most Italian dressmakers were happy to imitate Paris style, as were their counterparts in London and New York. Indeed, they boasted of their links with Paris, calling themselves by the French term 'atelier'. They employed French 'premières' (first hands), which testifies to the important role that France continued to play in Italian fashion. Thus the 'trickle down' nature of the dissemination of fashion in this period, meant that French fashion still led the whole of the Italian market, as it did the rest of the international fashion world.

By the end of the 1940s, most Italian houses had resumed the practice of sending designers to the Paris shows, or buying French styles from the translation agencies. This was explained by *WWD* in March 1950, which recorded that: 'all but a few of the Milan dressmakers, high style fabric firms and accessory houses have had their reps at the Paris showings, either to buy, as in the case of the dressmakers, or to sell – this is the fabric firms – or both to buy and sell, as do a few of the accessory firms'.

The Model House system described by Maria Pezzi quickly re-established its links with Paris soon after the War and this was reported in the same *WWD* article: 'First to hold openings are the so-called "model houses" which sell only to trade buyers or to trade and private clients both. Some in the latter group have a second showing later for private clients only.' It is also interesting to note that by this point that these Modellisti were also selling, in unknown quantities, to some foreign markets: 'Besides catering to the dressmakers from all over Italy who do not go to Paris themselves, the big Milan firms sell to trade buyers from surrounding countries. Austrian buyers have been here this season; Egypt and other Med countries, as well as Switzerland, are mentioned as buying models in Italy.' Whilst 'Italian style' may not yet have had an international allure, it seems that a combination of skill, price and value for money was already beginning to draw international trade.

Analysis of the Italian fashion magazine *Linea Italiana* clearly illustrates this typical Paris orientation in the late 1940s. There are articles on the latest Paris styles in each issue, including both photographic coverage and drawings of the Paris collections, such as 'Impressions of Paris' in the autumn 1948 edition. It is not unusual to see Italian fashion integrated on the pages along with the latest French couture styles, perhaps in the hope that some of the prestige would rub off. In the same issue, Vera Rossi comments on 'French fashion and ours: regrets and wishes'. This included photographs of the latest creations by French designers such as Dior and Fath, juxtaposed with others by Italian names such as Arano, Cerri, Tizzoni and Biki.

Some of the Italian garments featured are openly presented as Italian, but in many cases the name of the Italian 'designer' is printed alongside the source of direct Parisian inspiration. For example, figure 6 is a model which was sold by Italian couturier Galitzine, worn by the Countess Crespi, an Italian socialite and beauty, but was described as a 'modello Christian Dior' in the

Sumptuous Marucelli evening gown in azure and petrol-blue satin.
Described as a 'personal success', and 'entirely inspired by neo-classical
imperialism', rather than French style. Source: *Linea Italiana*, Autumn
1951, p. 59

Fontana scarlet evening gown, 1953, in draped soft silk crepe, with a
simple, curvaceous silhouette. Label reads 'Sorelle Fontana Roma'.
Source: Fontana archive, Rome, n.17/F 1953. Courtesy of Sorelle
Fontana, Alta Moda SRL.

Galitzine suit comprising a short, sleeveless, waisted cocktail dress and matching beaded jacket, c.1962. Label reads 'Irene Galitzine Roma'. Source: Pitti Palace, Florence, TA 3898/9. Courtesy of the Ministero per i Beni e le Attività Culturali. Further reproductions or duplications by any means are forbidden

Fontana strapless full-length evening gown in shaded pink and green rayon tulle, worn with pink gauntlets. Source: *Linea Italiana*, Autumn 1949, p. 29.

Antonelli Mini coat, dress and stockings suit. The coat is of navy wool in an orange, yellow and turquoise check weave, and is slightly fitted with a tailored collar, patch pocket, half-belt and four high buttons. The shift dress is of turquoise wool, with cap sleeves, a horizontal bust seam, and buttoned patch pockets. The stockings are bright orange. Label reads 'Antonelli Roma'. Source: Brighton Museum and Art Gallery, Ho 312/79, a, b, c.

Pucci silk skirt, mid-1950s, with a loose unstructured shape, bright colours and stylised pattern using US-inspired motifs. Worn by Mrs R.A. Vesty. Label reads 'Made in Italy, Fuilio, Capri SRL, Florence'. Source: Courtesy of the Museum of Costume, Bath, BATMCI. 42.98.

Brunelli ski-wear, comprising red-blouson and black trousers. Source: *Linea Italiana*, Winter 1949, p. 14.

15

Greider ski-wear, comprising yellow jumper, yellow and orange knitted hat, black gloves and ski-trousers. Source: *Linea Maglia*, Winter 1954, p. 29.

Figure 6. Galitzine evening dress, worn by the Countess Crespi, an Italian socialite and beauty and described as a 'modello Christian Dior'. Source: *Linea Italiana*, Summer 1948, p. 21.

summer 1948 edition. This means that either Galitzine was buying originals in Paris and simply reselling them in Italy (which was a known practice), or, more likely, had bought a toile or a pattern and was producing copies or adaptations. Evidently, either way, this represented excellent publicity value. Yet by autumn of that year, *Linea Italiana* claimed that Italian dressmakers were fed up with paying the high prices charged by French couturiers for the right to copy; some, they said, had paid 'incredible figures'.

In this same period there is also a marked increase of interest in the international place of Italian fashion. Even before the first collective shows in Florence in 1951, commentators began to notice both a conscious effort to move away from Paris dominance, and the emergence of a discernible Italian style. For example, following the liberation of Italy, but before the end of hostilities, the young and elegant editor of US *Vogue*, Bettina Ballard, visited Rome and wrote in her memoirs that she was astonished by the 'lovely, warm-skinned Roman women in their gay pretty print dresses . . . and Roman sandals' and felt instantly unfashionable.[6] Ballard recounts how she quickly found a local dressmaker 'to bring my civilian clothes up to Roman standards of fashion', and 'sent all the information I could to *Vogue* about the way the Romans lived and dressed and entertained'.

It is not surprising, therefore, that as early as January 1947, US *Vogue* 'covered the major fashion houses of Italy' in an article by Marya Mannes entitled 'The Fine Italian Hand'. This same article had been published in British *Vogue* in September the previous year, and offers an invaluable insight into the American perception of Italian style just after the War; this is crucial, because the US represented the major international market for fashion in these years. It begins with *Vogue*'s explanation of Italy's 'two great fashion advantages: wonderful materials and a seemingly inexhaustible pool of hand-labour'. The definition of Italian style begins: 'Italian clothes are inclined to be as extrovert as the people who wear them – gay, charming, sometimes dramatic, but seldom imaginative or arresting.' Mannes also states that 'it was difficult to discover any strong native current, except in the beach clothes'. This is a significant comment in view of the fact that Italian beach and leisure wear was so quickly to become of immense interest to foreign buyers. It is also significant that the competitiveness of Italian prices was already stressed: 'The price range in these houses hovered around 30,000 lire (£30) for a day dress and 60,000 for an evening gown. Certainly the prices are far lower than in Paris.' The attraction of the quality of Italy's fabrics, decoration and casual wear together with far lower price levels remains a recurrent theme in the reporting of Italian fashion in the 1950s.

The only complaint voiced in this early article concerned the level of surface decoration: 'the chief native weakness seems to be, in fact, a certain fussiness which extends even to their clothes, and which reduces the beauty of the fabrics themselves through unnecessary and extraneous detail'. The Mannes article concluded that 'Italy has everything necessary to a vital and original fashion industry – talent, fabric and plenty of beautiful women.' Perhaps the most significant comment of all, however, is the comment that 'with post-war easing of materials and labour and with, perhaps, more expert fashion direction than their local publications are prepared to give, Italian clothes should command a distinguished audience'. Since US *Vogue* was available in Italy at this point, and since Giorgini was well-acquainted with the American market, it is highly likely that he and others working in Italian fashion would have been well aware of this type of constructive criticism, and indeed of this particular piece, and reacted accordingly.

In fact, Italian fashion journalists were also devoting attention to stylistic emancipation from France, by this stage. *Bellezza*, continued to cover the French collections in detail, but simultaneously stressed the innovation of Italian wartime collections, and pointed out that there was little justification for 'pilgrimage to Paris' or copying foreign models. Interestingly, also noticeable are some peculiarly Italian 'peasant influences', in designs by, for example, Pirovano, Cerri, Lelia and Baruffaldi. These are predominantly dresses and separates incorporating traditional embroideries and lace-work. Although this cannot be deemed a high fashion stylistic alternative to Paris, such details were welcomed by certain foreign buyers for their quality and novelty, according to *Linea Italiana*.

Then, in April 1949, two years after the launch of Dior's New Look, an important fashion show was staged by Germana Marucelli in Milan. Marucelli's designs were inspired by Italy's historical and artistic heritage and, in particular, the Italian Renaissance, in a specific effort to disengage Italian fashion from French style. The clothes were described by *Bellezza* as 'practical, graceful and, above all, youthful, conceived for women who live active lives, free from every useless, decorative encumbrance' in contrast to the 'ornamental luxury' of French style. This report marks an important precedent in the determination of Italian style through Italian eyes.

According to *WWD*, it was Milanese dressmakers such as Marucelli who led the move towards stylistic innovation. A March 1950 report on Milan fashion published 'in view of the American trade interest in the Italian style market', declared for example, that 'there is original design being done in Milan, and more could be done if the demand warranted. Marucelli and Noberasko have been most often named in answer to my question of where original Italian designs could be bought. Both houses have sold to American buyers. Marucelli does not buy anything from Paris.' Marucelli's speciality was embroidered dresses and bold colour combinations. Illustrating her use of colours, in the same article *WWD* described a summer dance frock with a skirt made of two-inch folds of silk organdie, each a different colour. In total, eight colours were used to give a rainbow effect.

This conscious move away from Paris style towards Italian innovation represents an explicit indication of forthcoming stylistic developments, and was evidently already of great interest to the American fashion trade. This process continued at a major fashion show at the Teatro Pergola in Florence, in May 1950. In *Italian Metamorphosis 1943–68*, Valerie Steele describes how 'Mannequins emerged from reproductions of famous Renaissance paintings, to emphasise the connection between fashion and Italy's heritage of art and culture'.[7] However, the significance of this show must have been limited, because although it was collective, it was not commercial, and was not presented to foreign buyers.

Yet in the same month, a *WWD* report on Roman fashion noted that although Galitzine was still buying in Paris, 'she also believes that life in Italy calls for some special styling, particularly in the summer season when only the thinnest fabrics can be worn'. The report also explained that whilst Gattinoni was also still going to Paris, 'there are a number of these clothes which seem more particularly Italian, often because of the material'. The Carosa collection was singled out by *WWD* as 'the best example of the Italian liking for sheer stuffs and embroideries'. Together, these press reports outline the particular character of Italian couture which was to become increasingly apparent as the 1950s progressed. Clearly the Italian tradition of fine embroideries continued to play an important role in its made-to-measure clothing, but by the early 1950s it had come together with a notable use of colour and fine, high-quality, innovative Italian fabric.

During the 1950s, French haute couture found that a combination of overt protectionism and high prices was beginning to have a negative effect on exports. According to one French newspaper, by 1955, Paris couture prices had risen an estimated 3,000 per cent compared to their pre-war level, and the international market was growing a little tired of it.[8] This meant that with their relatively low prices, there was gap which, if they could manage to prize it open, the Italians might be able to fill. Furthermore, Valerie Steele states that whilst researching her book *Paris Fashion: a Cultural History*, she found ample evidence that 'Americans have long felt deeply ambivalent about French fashion'.[9] Steele explains that whilst Americans slavishly followed Paris style, they simultaneously resented the dictatorship. These problems were exacerbated by a dwindling private audience which increased reliance on trade customers and subsidiary ventures, such as ready-to-wear and perfume.[10]

By September 1965, it was estimated by the *New York Times* that there were only 3,000 private customers for the thirty-eight remaining French houses. Whilst there is no evidence that the incomes of the very rich had fallen, their lifestyles had clearly irrevocably altered. Busy wealthy women were no longer prepared to spend so much of the necessary time required to fit made-to-measure clothes, nor did their social calendars demand it. Nonetheless, it must be stressed that despite these gradual changes, at the start of the 1950s, most Italian dressmakers still went to the Paris collections, and continued to reflect their influence. An example of this practice can be found in *Bellezza* in 1954, in an advertisement for the dressmaker 'Toninelli of Milan'. Toninelli was a well-known name, with salons in Rome, Florence and Milan. The spring/summer collection is illustrated with identified shots of models by French designers Fath and Dior.

Italian Couture Style 1951–65

Whilst the now famous first collective presentation of Italian fashion in 1951 (organised by Giorgini and discussed in chapter 2), was evidently not the first attempt to promote an Italian fashion industry, it marks both an awakening of international consciousness, and a very deliberate effort to sever stylistic links with Paris. Italian couturier Micol Fontana recalls that in return for his financial and organisational input, Giorgini demanded that there would be 'no more going to Paris', and no more imitation of French designs. Fontana says that this represented a request to literally 'sever their lifeline', because of course, all wealthy Italian ladies traditionally wanted French style. In this particular company there followed a period of intense and difficult deliberation amongst the Fontana sisters, with Zoè and Giovanna arguing for continued adherence to Paris style, and Micol for participation in Giorgini's show, before the final decision to take part was reached. The move represented a considerable risk. In effect, they were setting up in direct competition with France.

Fontana confirms that 1951 was the moment when Italian style emerged on the international stage. Nonetheless, it should not be assumed that all Italian couturiers suddenly forgot Paris and designed entirely independently thereafter. There was no abrupt break from the international dominance of Paris style at couture level, and adherence to the overall stylistic prescriptions of Paris continued unavoidably throughout the 1950s and early 1960s. In this period, the fashionable silhouette changed seasonally, disseminated from French couture houses to the entire international fashion system. Dior's well-publicised looks, such as the A line, and the H line were followed in a broad sense by all the Italian couture houses. The Italian move away from Paris may have gathered momentum from 1951, but it was not consistent at all levels of production and with all designers, and was seen less in terms of silhouette, than in use of colour, fabric and surface decoration.

However, it is significant that although the French collections continued to be covered by Italian fashion magazines, after 1951 a shift in the balance of coverage is clearly discernible. Although reference to Paris was still manifest, links between Italian designers and Paris fashion (which were stressed in the Italian fashion press before 1951) are difficult to find after this date, whilst the reporting of Italian fashion becomes increasingly prominent. For example, the autumn 1951 issue of *Linea Italiana* is subtitled 'Moda Italiana e Parigina', which, if anything, gives Italian fashion greater precedence over Paris. As well as the usual 'Letter from Paris', there is coverage of the 'second

Figure 7. Sumptuous Marucelli evening gown in azure and petrol-blue satin. Described as a 'personal success', and 'entirely inspired by neo-classical imperialism', rather than French style. Source: *Linea Italiana*, Autumn 1951, p. 59.

presentation of Italian high fashion to the Americans, from 19–21 July', which it records as 'an undeniable success', with 350 'quality' American buyers and journalists. As well as listing the key stores, the article mentions radio interviews, television transmissions and cinema reports, and states that the Italian collections preceded the 'sacred Paris presentations, at the explicit wish of the Americans'.

This 1951 report also describes the individual collections of each Italian designer, stressing where individuality and originality were to be seen, as at Carosa and Marucelli, for example. Figure 7 illustrates a sumptuous evening

Figure 8. Fontana couture wool suit, with loose-fitting jacket and contrast panels.
Source: *Linea Italiana*, Autumn 1951, p. 54.

gown in azure and petrol-blue satin by Marucelli, described as a 'personal success', 'entirely inspired by neo-classical imperialism', rather than French style, which, it was said, 'confirmed the courageousness of Italian fashion'. Also stressed is purity of line, and tailoring rigour, as in the Fontana example seen in figure 8. A few months later, in July 1952, *WWD* pinpointed Marucelli again, remarking that 'Marucelli displays the greatest independent creativeness and consistent development.' Evidence of Marucelli's individual style can be found in the exhibits chosen for the 1994 Italian Metamorphosis exhibition in New York.[11] Two short organza evening dresses from the early 1950s were displayed, both decorated with handpainted designs by Italian painter Giuseppe Capogrossi. The designs are high-waisted, with braided full double skirts, and bodice embroidery which echo the peasant inspiration of the fascist Ente.

Carla Strini, who was 'Head of Foreign Operations' at Pucci, attended the very first collective Italian fashion show in 1951. She remembers the embroideries, fabrics and colours particularly vividly, and says, for example, that 'the colours were very striking, especially the soft pastels of green and aqua which was very unusual'. She also states that 'the creativity of Italian textiles was determinant' into the formation of Italian style. Micol Fontana echoes these statements, saying that 'Italian couture was simpler in line. Draping good quality soft materials was an important part of this, but the real secret was in hidden construction; the garments were very carefully cut, but this was not shown.'

These specific design points are exemplified by examination of ten evening garments selected from museum and private collections. Italian evening wear was the most important export sector of Italian couture in this period, and typically followed the lines of Dior's New Look, which prescribed small shoulders (or strapless), a narrow waist, and either a very full or a very narrow skirt for evening wear. However, there are few Italian examples as extreme as most Paris designs and the following illustrations represent the typically moderated Italian interpretation.

The first example is a startling scarlet evening gown designed by Fontana in 1953, in draped soft crepe chiffon, with a simple, curvaceous silhouette (figure 9). According to Micol Fontana, it was vital that the gown fitted the individual body perfectly without discomfort. The structure (figure 10) is very intricate, with a firmly boned silk underbodice. Simple lines, with or without surface decoration and sumptuous use of colour gradually became the speciality of Italian fashion in the post-war period. This can be seen clearly in a US *Vogue* article, from April 1961, entitled, 'The Good Word on Italy and Italian Fashion' which comments that 'it was in colour, rather than in innovations of cut, that these collections made the news'. Examples cited include 'Capucci's tangerine-orange wool coat' and Pucci, who 'even made his models wear pink shoes and stockings'.

The second example of Italian style was designed by Galitzine in approximately 1962, and is particularly interesting because two variations of this outfit are held in museum collections, one at the Pitti Palace in Florence and one at the Victoria and Albert Museum in London.[12] The first is a suit comprising a short, sleeveless, waisted cocktail dress with a matching beaded jacket (figure 11). The fabric is particularly striking, an exotically coloured and patterned satin, with stylised flowers, leaves and butterflies, which incorporates both pastels and brights. The dress is lined with loose salmon-coloured silk and carefully finished, with a hand-sewn and weighted hem. The jacket is very

Figure 9. Fontana scarlet evening gown, 1953, in draped soft silk crepe, with a
simple, curvaceous silhouette. Label reads 'Sorelle Fontana Roma'.
Source: Fontana archive, Rome, n.17/F 1953. Courtesy of Sorelle
Fontana, Alta Moda SRL.

heavily beaded in accordance with the fabric pattern and lined with fine
green crepe de chine. There is great attention to detail; even the internal
poppers are covered with different colour crepe to match the fabric beneath.
The second variation is a three-piece and includes the same jacket, but is
matched with both green 'Capri pant' trousers, and a maxi wrap-around
over-skirt in the same fabric as the aforementioned dress, and shows an
aptitude for combining elegance with practicality. This ensemble demonstrates
thoughtful use of surface decoration, colour, texture and pattern and is an
excellent example of the contribution of fabric pattern to the form of Italian
couture in these years.

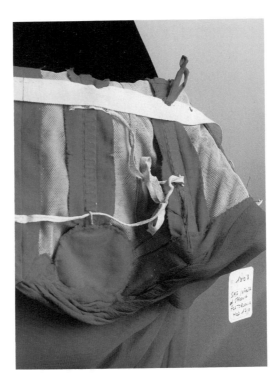

Figure 10. The firmly boned silk underbodice of figure 9, showing the typically intricate structure of Italian couture evening wear. Source: Fontana archive, Rome, n.17/F 1953. Courtesy of Sorelle Fontana, Alta Moda SRL.

Although French couturiers used intricate hand-worked beading in the 1950s and early 1960s, such decoration was already long known as an Italian specialisation, reflecting Italy's reputation for exquisite craftsmanship. Besides the above jacket by Galitzine, there are numerous surviving examples from the 1950s and early 1960s in museum collections and the M. H. De Young Memorial Museum in San Francisco has several fine examples. Again, these garments are all made from fine silk fabrics, which were a well-known specialisation of the Italian textile industry.

The earliest is a cream satin evening gown by Ferrario of 1949, which was worn by Naz Mardikian, an Armenian émigré involved with the Italian Resistance during the War, who was very keen to help resurrect Italian industry after the War.[13] Naz Mardikian was given a ball gown every year by Ferrario in recognition for her efforts.[14] This one was worn at the 1949 opening of the San Francisco opera, a major social and sartorial event in the city's calendar.

Figure 11. Galitzine suit comprising a short, sleeveless, waisted cocktail dress and matching beaded jacket, c.1962. Label reads 'Irene Galitzine Roma'. Source: Pitti Palace, Florence, TA 3898/9. Courtesy of the Ministero per i Beni e le Attività Culturali. Further reproductions or duplications by any means are forbidden.

It is decorated with all-over scrolled embroidery using toning silk thread, cream sequins and amber glass. The front has a false-wrap which suggests it was meant to swing open as the wearer walked, perhaps offering a glimpse of the lower leg. Another example from this collection was also worn by Naz Mardikian for the same occasion about seven years later (figure 12).

Figure 12. Ferrario evening gown, 1949. Worn strapless and full length, in royal blue satin, covered with stylised floral and 'fleur de lys' embroidery, using gold thread, bugle beads, blue sequins and blue and amber glass. Worn with matching embroidered stole. Label reads 'Ferrario Milano'. Source: Fine Arts Museums of San Francisco, gift of Anita Naz Mardikian, 1991.83.2a–b.

This dress is also by Ferrario, and is noticeably similar. It is strapless and full length, in royal blue satin, and is covered with stylised floral and *fleur de lys* embroidery, using gold thread, bugle beads, blue sequins and blue and amber glass.

Naz Mardikian was not the only San Francisco resident to wear embroidered Italian eveningwear. The De Young Museum also has a beige silk shantung cocktail dress by the couturier Simonetta, dating from the late

1950s, which was worn by Mrs John Rosekrans Junior for her second wedding.[15] This gown is short with small sleeves, but the bodice is nonetheless encrusted by paste beads and chenille embroidery, in floral pattern. 'Dodie' Rosekrans apparently 'had a broad physique, so puffy styles suited her especially well'.[16] There are a number of Simonetta garments in this collection, worn until the mid-1960s by the same donor. Now in her seventies, Dodie Rosekrans was well-known in post-war San Francisco society for her independent sense of fashion. Italian fashion appealed to her, because it was unusual, contemporary and colourful. This can also be seen in a second Rosekrans donation, a 1957–8 short cocktail dress also by Simonetta, which is an excellent example of the power of colour in Italian fabrics (figure 13).[17] The heavy silk satin is warp-printed, with large blue roses on an aqua background. The cut is intricate, with a short raised belt at centre-front, and a sack-back. It is not known where Dodie Rosekrans purchased her Italian outfits, but it is likely that they were either purchased in Italy or from top San Francisco department store, I Magnin, which, as with other elite US stores discussed in chapter 2, was then importing top Italian fashion.

Three further evening wear examples of note include a jacket in the collection of the Fashion Institute of Design and Merchandising, Los Angeles, and two dresses at the Victoria and Albert Museum, London. Although these garments have not been firmly dated, they are all knee-length and without a defined waist, in the style of the late 1950s-early 1960s. They are important because of their combination of simple cut and surface decoration. The first is a short cream satin evening coat by Tiziani, unfitted with a round neck (figure 14). The cut and colour contrast with the striking black geometric sequinned decoration, and black buttons. The second is a cream sleeveless dress by Fabiani, which is decorated only by a horizontal diamond of clear beads and silver sequins at the centre waist, the only clear indication that the dress was designed as evening wear.[18] The third is a short evening dress by Fantechi, which indicates that total surface decoration used in conjunction with fabric pattern, continued in Italian evening wear, but in a less formal way than in the early post war-years.[19] In this uncomplicated, sleeveless, shift-dress of 1959, shape contrasts with the large-scale floral pattern, vibrant colour, and beaded and sequinned decoration. The dress is made of silk with printed orange flowers on a pale blue ground and an organza lining. The entire surface is covered with lines of vertically sewn clear sequins and the pattern is emphasised with drops of tiny coloured glass beads, effecting a glamorous but much more relaxed look than the examples of the early 1950s.

These three short evening dresses suggest that whilst the surface decoration of Italian couture grew less detailed and curvilinear in the late 1950s, it retained its significance for the simpler shapes of the period. Seen collectively,

Figure 13. Simonetta cocktail dress, 1957–8. An excellent example of the power
of colour in Italian fabrics. The heavy satin is warp-printed, with large
blue roses on an aqua background. The cut is intricate, with a short
raised belt at centre-front, and a sack-back. Label reads 'Simonetta
Roma'. Source: Fine Arts Museums of San Francisco, gift of Mrs John
Rosekrans Jnr., 1983.36.30.

the total ten evening garments offer important evidence of Italian use of
colour, fabric, surface decoration, and simple lines, all of which were already
beginning to distance Italian fashion style from that of Paris couture.

This reading is substantiated by the contemporary press. Two early examples
can be found in *Linea Italiana* in 1949. Firstly, a green and white appliquéd
organza evening gown by Veneziani (figure 15), and secondly, a sumptuous
strapless evening gown by Fontana, in pink and green shaded rayon tulle,
which is decorated with large three-dimensional flowers and worn with long,

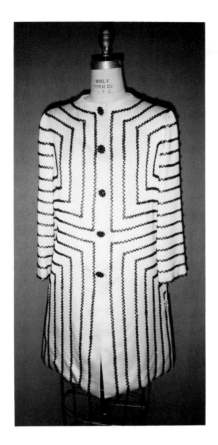

Figure 14. Tiziani short cream satin evening coat, unfitted with a round neck, late
1950s–early 1960s. The cut and colour contrast with the striking black
geometric sequinned decoration, and black buttons. Label reads
'Tiziani Roma'. Source: In the collection of the FIDM Museum and
Library Foundation, Los Angeles, 86-1960-064.1 TIZI.

soft pink gauntlets (figure 16). In summer 1954, *Linea Maglia* included a
full-page editorial featuring a halter-neck full-length evening gown in white
tulle and satin by couturier Antonelli, decorated with panels of silver and
red embroidery (figure 17). Four years later, the spring 1958 issue included a
strapless cocktail dress by Fercioni, in two tones of azure blue with a border
of white stylised swans (figure 18), as well as an elegant white organdie dress
by Vanna, with a full skirt and strapless fitted bodice, stamped in a floral
design and worn with a green cape and gloves, which was shot dramatically
at the Italian lakeside, under a weeping willow (figure 19). These three

Figure 15. Veneziani green and white organza strapless full-length evening gown, with appliqué embroidery. Source: *Linea Italiana*, Summer 1949, p. 17.

examples underline the key characteristics which were evolving in Italian couture evening wear: gowns in simple, elegant, and seasonally stylish shapes which used pattern, fabric and colour to emphasise the dramatic effect.

The US trade perspective seen in *WWD* reports of the couture collections from the early 1950s corroborates this assessment of Italian couture 'special-isation' in three key ways. Particular attention is given to evening wear, intricate surface decoration, and colourful fabrics. For example, in December 1951 'floor length gowns, rich fabrics – here is a cross-section of evening gowns' were observed. In the following January it was noted that 'richly embroidered evening gowns . . . fabrics play a big role in fashion interest in these showings', and later that month came the headline 'Italian evening gowns win buyers' praise'.

Although Italian couture became increasingly well-known for its evening wear, formal day dress was also always produced and sold successfully in

Figure 16. Fontana strapless full-length evening gown in shaded pink and green rayon tulle, worn with pink gauntlets. Source: *Linea Italiana*, Autumn 1949, p. 29.

the US. Broadly, like the evening wear, daywear followed the Paris 'New Look'. Figure 20 is an example featured in a *Linea Italiana* editorial in spring 1951, a tailored black and grey stripe suit by Paris couturier Jean Dessès. Figure 21 is a spring 1951 tailored rayon suit by the Italian Baruffaldi. It is clear that this is a softer, more wearable garment than the typically more extreme French style of the same date seen in the previous illustration, and it was this softer look which the domestic and US markets found so appealing.

Few examples of Italian couture daywear survive in museum collections, probably because historically, donors and curators have not felt them worthy of collection; donors may also have worn them far more, which may have damaged them and made them less collectable. The only daywear examples found are in the Fashion Institute of Design and Merchandising (FIDM) collection in Los Angeles, the Brighton Museum and Art Gallery and the V&A, London, and date from the mid-1960s. They comprise two dresses,

Figure 17. Antonelli halter neck full-length grand evening gown in white tulle and satin, with silver and red embroidered panels. Source: *Linea Italiana*, Summer 1954, p. 35.

and three dress-jacket/coat suits. The first is a Tiziani day dress in brown wool, sleeveless and without decoration but enlivened by semi-circular gores and buttoned belt tabs at the front waist (figure 22). The second outfit is also by Tiziani, and comprises a short dress with matching jacket (figure 23). The dress has a navy blue top which is broken up by two vertical stripes of patterned beige knit and an a-line beige skirt. The five-buttoned jacket is semi-fitted, with slightly full cuffed sleeves and a round neck.

The next example of Italian daywear found in museum collections is another bold dress-suit by Fabiani, circa 1965.[20] This suit is in a very heavy woven wool, with navy and red horizontal stripes. It consists of a double-breasted unfitted jacket, with a rounded collar, and a shift-dress with a high waist and a cream silk sleeveless bodice. The final two examples were both worn by an English woman married to an Italian, Mrs Brenda Azario, who donated them to the Brighton collection and dated them precisely to 1965. The first is a heavy 'mini-dress' by Mila Schön, a slightly flared shift, fastened at the side with six large white plastic buttons (figure 24). It is made in double-

Figure 18. Fercioni strapless cocktail dress, in two tones of azure blue with a border of white stylised swans. Source: *Linea Italiana*, Spring 1954, p. 17.

sided woven wool, with a turquoise ground and wide vertical navy stripes, and bands of white at the centre-front and centre-back. The second is a 'mini' coat, dress and stockings suit by Antonelli (figure 25). The coat is of navy blue wool in an orange, yellow and turquoise check weave, and is slightly fitted with a tailored collar, an unusual cutaway v-shape patch pocket, a half-belt and four high buttons. The shift dress is of turquoise blue wool, with cap sleeves, a horizontal bust seam, and buttoned patch pockets. The matching stockings are a very bright orange. Of all the ensembles described, this outfit is perhaps the most visually striking because of the juxtaposition of vivid colours, with simple shapes. All the daywear examples seem soft and easy, compared to the sharp French tailoring.

The daywear featured in the contemporary press further emphasised these factors. The broad spectrum of Italian garments featured in *Linea Italiana*, for example, remains through the mid-1950s, and the general trend towards 'easy elegance' continued; there are simple box-shape suits with sparse detailing, except perhaps a turned back cuff, and a matching hat (as in figure 26).

Figure 19. Vanna white organdie floral printed evening dress, with a full skirt and strapless fitted bodice, stamped in a floral design and worn with a green velvet cape and white gloves. Source: *Linea Maglia*, Summer 1954, p. 29.

In the light of this interpretation, it is interesting that in April 1961 US *Vogue* typically chose to emphasise Italian use of colour, rather than its subtle cuts. An article entitled 'The good word on Italy and Italian Fashion', reported that in the Florentine collections, 'it was colour, rather than innovations of cut' that made the news. The article prosaically explained that 'there were apricots in every shade of ripeness, pinks in every blush of pinkness, strawberry and camellia reds, pale blue and periwinkle blue, pistache and jade greens, oranges, yellows, bronzes. Coats and capes were often reversible, a different colour on each side – an apricot shantung coat, for example, reversing to pale-blue shantung. Or another colour was introduced in bandings or insets – Capucci's tangerine-orange wool coat had broad inset bands of dark-bronze wool. Also at Capucci: dresses made entirely of multi-coloured ribbons woven dazzlingly together.' This was illustrated by photographs of examples, including the aforementioned cape by Capucci, Italian couture's

Figure 20. Tailored black and grey stripe suit by Paris couturier Jean Dessès, following the Paris 'New Look' line established by Dior in the late 1940s. Source: *Linea Italiana*, Spring 1951, p. 58.

rising new star. It is described as 'one of Capucci's fashion triumphs'. This use of strong vibrant colour predates that of London and Paris, and, as we have seen, became an important part of Italian fashion style early in its development. Of course, Italian designers did not restrict themselves to bright hues. Another daywear example illustrated in this article is a loose coat by Fabiani, 'that's camel-coloured on one side, charcoal-grey on the other'.

In *WWD* there are very few references to couture daywear, in contrast to its coverage of evening wear, and this reflects the export market for Italian couture. In January 1952, 'simple daytime suits' were noted, whilst 'manufacturers liked the day clothes because they simplified current silhouettes adapted to the average woman,' and in August 1956, 'classic constructed coats and suits from Guidi' were applauded. However, it is highly significant that detailed accounts of Italian couture of any type grow scarce in *WWD* from this point, in contrast to increasing coverage of the ready-to-wear

Figure 21. Baruffaldi suit with a maroon rayon jacket, a softer, more wearable garment than the typically more extreme French style of the same date seen in the previous illustration. Source: *Linea Italiana*, Spring 1951, p. 61.

boutique collections. One January 1957 report typifies this shift, describing 'couture styles, including a group of lavishly embroidered items from Veneziani, Antonelli and Schuberth', under the title 'US record set on sportswear buying in Italy'.

Italian Boutique Style 1951–65

It has already been shown that just below the level of made-to-measure couture, boutique fashions had been produced in Italy and sold abroad in the late 1940s, but it was not until the Florentine shows from 1951 that collections began to be presented to an international audience of buyers and press. Gianni Ghini, who was present at these early boutique collections, defines boutique fashion as 'different, novel and fantastic, though not extreme. It was also comfortable, simple and more wearable than the couture. Fabric

Figure 22. Tiziani day dress in brown wool, mid-1960s, sleeveless and without decoration but enlivened by semi-circular gores and buttoned belt tabs at the front waist. Label reads 'Tiziani Roma'. Source: In the collection of the FIDM Museum and Library Foundation, Los Angeles, 84-1967.008.21 TIZI.

and colours were important.' Ghini also makes the important point that 'it was much easier for the press to state that the boutique was innovative, because the French did not have it'. By this he means that the boutique market was seen to contrast with the grand formality of French couture. As such, boutique style represented a niche which Italy could carve out in the international market, without standing in direct competition to Paris, or copying it.

Figure 23. Tiziani suit comprising a short dress with matching jacket, mid-1960s. The dress has a navy blue top which is broken up by two vertical stripes of patterned beige knit and an a-line beige skirt. The jacket is semi-fitted, with slightly full cuffed sleeves and a round neck. Label reads 'Tiziani Roma'. Source: In the collection of the FIDM Museum and Library Foundation, Los Angeles, 84-1968.010.10 TIZI.

Even in the 1950s, according to Italian fashion PR Luigi Settembrini, 'Italians stood out for their greater simplicity.'[21] Settembrini stresses that 'features like wearability, practicality, and simple cut were even more pronounced in the boutique collections which accompanied the high fashion showings. They were also more in tune with the "modern woman", especially the American woman who was understood to be active and working.' He continues: 'It is these collections that represent a truly new understanding of how women dress. They were also forums for freer experimentation, in material, production and cut.' The most frequently cited example of such experimentation in the contemporary press is Pucci's casual jersey printwear.

It is generally accepted that Pucci was the first and most successful Italian boutique designer in the two decades after the Second World War. With great

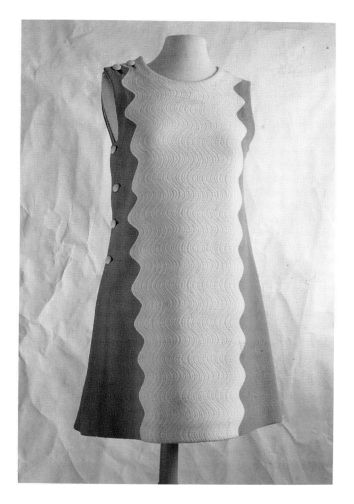

Figure 24. Mila Schön mini-dress, 1965. Heavy turquoise wool shift, with wide vertical navy stripes, and bands of white at the centre-front and centre-back and side-fastened with six large white plastic buttons. Worn by Mrs Brenda Azario. Label reads 'Mila Schön, Italia'. Source: Brighton Museum and Art Gallery, Ho 313/79.

fervour, his ex-employee Carla Strini, claims that 'Pucci didn't just create Italian sportswear, he created sportswear, period. Before this, sportswear had meant a combination of slacks or skirts with tops and blouses. Pucci linked it with sport and made it fun.'[22] Strini cites Pucci's ski-pants, his first garment, in support of this. She says that earlier ski-pants were 'unflattering and baggy garments' which made 'women look like a bag rolling downhill'. She explains that Pucci created 'tight flattering ones, which women could look good in'.

Figure 25. Antonelli Mini coat, dress and stockings suit. The coat is of navy wool in an orange, yellow and turquoise check weave, and is slightly fitted with a tailored collar, patch pocket, half-belt and four high buttons. The shift dress is of turquoise wool, with cap sleeves, a horizontal bust seam, and buttoned patch pockets. The stockings are bright orange. Label reads 'Antonelli Roma'. Source: Brighton Museum and Art Gallery, Ho 312/79, a, b, c.

This new approach to shape was combined with unfamiliar colours and patterns, and unexpected fabrics such as light silk jersey, which were easy to wear and care for. Pucci's signature garments were narrow Capri pants, loose, long, square-cut, silk jersey shirts, and pared-down shirt-dresses, all in unusual brightly coloured prints. They were seen as sensual, slinky, sleek and slender, as well as relaxed, elegant and very flattering. Certainly, the clothes and the lifestyle for which they were designed were very different from the restrictive and formal designs of contemporary Paris fashion.

Figure 26. Carosa simple pink and grey stripe box-shape suit, with sparse detailing, except a turned-back cuff, and a matching hat. Source: *Linea Italiana*, Spring 1955, p. 71.

Whilst it must be remembered that these garments were very expensive (and were beyond the reach of all but the wealthy), for the international jet-set, Pucci's easy-to-pack designs became symbols of lifestyle and exclusivity. The fashion editor of US magazine *Life* summed it up in August 1951, when she wrote that: 'Pucci made it chic to be casual, with his aristocratic sportswear designs.' This sentiment was echoed by US *Vogue*'s Bettina Ballard, who wrote that 'Possibly what Italy has contributed of the most universal fashion value is their sportswear. The individual who has done the most to make the Italian sports look fashionable is Emilio Pucci.'[23]

There are more surviving Pucci garments in museum and private collections than by any other Italian designer, at either couture or boutique level. For example, the Museum of the City of New York has eight Pucci pieces thought to pre-date 1966, but only two other garments by other Italian designers.[24] The Fashion Institute of Technology Costume Collection, in New York, has twenty-seven Pucci garments dating from the 1950s, and a massive eighty-seven from the 1960s, and there are many other examples of Pucci's work in other collections.[25] These numbers testify to the increasing popularity of Pucci in America in these years. There are far fewer in Britain, but Bath Costume Museum has three Pucci shirts dating from the 1950s and 1960s, worn by a well-known local lady called Mrs R.A. Vestey. One of these, from the mid-1950s, is shown in figure 27, and is typical in its loose unstructured shape, bright colours and stylised pattern. Particularly interesting here are the US-inspired motifs, such as Native American mermaids, and place names such as San Francisco and Nevada.

Bath Costume Museum also has a boutique outfit by Antonelli which is described as a 'ski-suit', but which was probably worn for informal winter-wear (figure 28). It dates from the mid-1950s and consists of an unfitted wool/synthetic jacket, strawberry-pink rollneck sweater and ski-pants and was worn with matching cloth boots. Clearly, this relaxed look contrasts very sharply with the approach of contemporary French couture. A Simonetta Sport trouser suit held in the V&A collection, shows how the look extended into the early 1960s.[26] This suit comprises a long sleeve sweater with a roll-collar and ribbed flounces at the cuff, and plain wide-leg trousers with an elasticated waistband. The fabric is dark blue synthetic jersey, the garment is unfitted, and the overall effect is of the easy elegance described by *Life* magazine.

A rather more prim, yet still spare Italian boutique design can be seen in figure 29. This is a semi-fitted day coat worn by Giovanna, one of the three Fontana sisters, and made in 1964, under the 'Fontana Alta Moda Pronta' (Fontana High Fashion Ready-to-Wear) label. With its thick wool in plain grey and a geometric monochrome design, the coat makes striking use of fabric pattern, through its simple construction, and an uncluttered line. The fastenings are simple black buttons with a gold rim. This approach, combining simple form with unusual details or fabric treatment, can also be seen in three illustrations of Fontana boutique, found in the photographic records of the Fontana archive.

Figure 30 shows a day dress from the autumn-winter 1962/3 collection, a plain shift in what appears to be two colours of fine wool. The interest is centred on the intersection of the two fabrics at low waist height, and the neck, both of which are marked by a row of drop circles. The second photograph (figure 31) is from the same collection, a short evening dress in plain fabric which is entirely unadorned. Here the focus is at the waist, which is nipped-in using an asymmetric twisted drape, with an overhanging bodice. The third photograph (figure 32) was shot in the Piazza di Spagna, Rome, a few yards from the Fontana atelier, and is from the spring-summer boutique collection of 1964. The two day dresses shown are both simple shifts, in two

Figure 27. Pucci silk shirt, mid-1950s, with a loose unstructured shape, bright
colours and stylised pattern using US-inspired motifs. Worn by Mrs
R.A. Vestey. Label reads 'Made in Italy, Fuilio, Capri SRL, Florence'.
Source: Courtesy of the Museum of Costume, Bath, BATMCI. 42.98.

different colours, which use drawn detail, simulated to indicate buttons and
seams, in the Surrealist manner.[27] All three examples contribute to the
definition of Italian boutique style; the designs are restrained, yet offer detail
which catches the eye, at sub-couture prices.

Stylistic analysis of Italian boutique designs is also possible through con-
sideration of the garments presented at the Pitti Palace in July 1952, which
have been preserved on a contemporary film entitled 'La Settimana Incom:
Moda a Palazzo Pitti'.[28] The black and white film includes boutique collections with skirts, organza overshirts and slacks in wide colour blocks, with

Figure 28. Antonelli 'ski-suit', mid-1950s comprising a wool/ synthetic mix unfitted jacket and ski-pants, and pink rollneck sweater, which was worn with matching cloth boots. Labels read 'Antonelli Roma' and 'Made in Italy'. Source: Courtesy of the Museum of Costume, Bath, BATMC 94.180 to B.

some bold flower prints. Perhaps the most important factor is the obvious versatility of the outfits, which is clearly a selling point; for example, skirts are removed to reveal tight Capri pants, for multi-functional use.

Since there is such a narrow range of surviving Italian boutique wear, contemporary media coverage is especially important in a reading of style at this level of production. *Bellezza* covered Italian boutique from the late 1940s. For example, an April 1948 article reported 'At the scene of the Italian collections', featuring daywear from boutique designers Vanna and Fiorani,

Figure 29. Fontana semi-fitted daycoat, 1964. Striking use is made of fabric pattern through the combination of thick wool in plain grey, a geometric monochrome design and an uncluttered line. Worn by Giovanna, one of the three Fontana sisters. Label reads 'Fontana Alta Moda Pronta'. Source: Fontana archive, Rome, n.31/F. Courtesy of Sorelle Fontana, Alta Moda SRL.

drawn by the famous Italian illustrator Brunetta, as well as one on beachwear entitled 'The Islands'. Another typical example of *Bellezza*'s interest in casual outdoor garb was published in July 1953, and was called 'The Wind on the Beach'. This piece included beach shots of a young model with loose hair and no shoes, wearing a jersey two-piece (trousers and a loose stripe top) by Simonetta, and a halter top by Antonelli, worn with shorts (figure 33). Simonetta and Antonelli were both couture designers with boutique ranges.

Figure 30. Fontana daydress, a plain shift in what appears to be two colours of
fine wool. The interest is centred on the intersection of the two fabrics
at low waist height, and the neck, both of which are marked by a row of
drop circles. 'Collezione Boutique Autunno-Inverno 1962/1963'.
Source: Fontana archive, Rome, photographic records. Courtesy of
Sorelle Fontana, Alta Moda SRL.

The stress on outdoor life and elegant, easy and youthful ready-to-wear
clothing is seen again, for example, the following winter, in January 1954,
when *Bellezza* featured 'A Beautiful Surprise in Easy Solutions.' The surprise
consisted of narrow trousers tucked into flat ankle boots, worn with roll-
neck jumpers and a fringed check wool jacket by 'sportswear house' Boutique
4 Spilling (figure 34). These garments were hailed as 'the ultimate find of
the season', giving 'ample freedom of movement and an impeccable line'. In
July 1959 *Bellezza* featured a boutique designer called Krizia, who was later
to become very important in the development of the Milanese high fashion
ready-to-wear industry. In an article entitled 'Sport-Knitwear', Krizia's 'jumpsuit' in dog-tooth check was worn with a sleeveless mohair jerkin (figure 35)
and points towards the easy shapes for which Italian fashion has become so
well known.

Figure 31. Fontana unadorned short evening dress in plain fabric. The focus is at the waist, which is nipped-in using an asymmetric twisted drape, over which the bodice hangs. 'Collezione Boutique Autunno-Inverno 1962/1963'. Source: Fontana archive, Rome, photographic records. Courtesy of Sorelle Fontana, Alta Moda SRL.

Boutique coverage by *Linea Italiana* magazine began in winter 1949 with a feature for ski resort-wear, entitled 'Sport below Zero'. The article included garments by sportswear label Brunelli (figure 36) and like *Bellezza*'s coverage, indicates an early emphasis on the outdoor and the casual. *Linea Italiana* featured swimwear and beachwear for the first time that summer, with items by both well-known couture houses such as Veneziani, and a number of sportswear firms such as Lilian. There is an array of outdoor settings, on deck, on the quayside, and on the beach. Young girls are seen at the seaside dressed in afternoon dresses, playsuits, smocks, Capri pants, wraps, bikinis, and hooded tops (figure 37). The red and green striped playsuit seen in figure 38 was designed by Mirsa five years later, in 1956, and is another excellent example of the 'easy' elegance of Italian beachwear style.[29] Winter leisure wear continued to be featured regularly. One chic example is seen in figure

Figure 32. Fontana simple shift day dresses in two different colours, decorated with drawn detail, simulated to indicate buttons and seams, in the Surrealist manner. Shot in the Piazza di Spagna, Rome, a few yards from the Fontana atelier. 'Collezione Boutique Primavera-Estate 1964'. Source: Fontana archive, Rome, photographic records. Courtesy of Sorelle Fontana, Alta Moda SRL.

39, a bright yellow jumper with a double ring collar in Marzotto wool by Greider, which was worn with a matching yellow and orange knitted hat, black gloves and ski-trousers.

In these years, editorials continue to stress both the elegance and the utility of the garments; trousers are hailed for their crease-resistance, as well as the way they 'do not spoil grace and femininity'.[30] Designs for short checked trousers by Brunelli were applauded for connecting elegance and practicality. Veneziani's new boutique label was exalted for its 'new level of ideas and spirit', an example of which is seen in figure 40, 'an unfitted chamois leather jacket by Veneziani-Sport'.[31] This was certainly an expensive garment, but it was not made-to-measure, and was at the forefront of the new Italian trend towards casual sportswear. It is significant that the key words 'easeful

Figure 33. Simonetta jersey two-piece (trousers and a loose stripe top), and a halter top by Antonelli, worn with shorts and narrow trousers. Source: *Bellezza*, July 1953, pp. 22–3.

grace,' used as early as 1951, have become increasingly synonymous with 'Italian style' in the years since the Second World War.

An important subset of the boutique sector, which fits this description very neatly, was Italy's fashion knitwear, which has already been discussed in chapter 2. In summer 1954, the knitwear magazine *Linea Maglia*, published an editorial entitled 'Holiday knitwear synthesised for the modern taste'. The feature includes swimming costumes and other beachwear, including Emilio Pucci's printed 'fishtail' cotton Capri pants and thong sandals, worn with a fisherman-style jumper and set against a backdrop of boats and fishermen (figure 41). The article concludes that 'knitwear is an ideal complement to today's wardrobe' and 'is the basis of the sporting wardrobe in every season' as well as being 'the ultimate news in elegance, which, for its line and colour fits in well with high fashion'. Elegance, colour and practicality are the key selling points.

Figure 34. Boutique 4 Spilling narrow trousers tucked into flat ankle boots, worn with roll-neck jumpers and a fringed check wool jacket. Source: *Bellezza*, January 1954, pp. 62–3.

In the Italian fashion industry's search for innovative dual-purpose clothing, it is clear that as well as being well-suited to outdoor leisure pursuits, knitwear could also bridge the gap between formal and informal wear, with outfits that offered elegance and some forms of surface decoration, as well as ease and comfort. This ethos was taken one step further in a 1955 editorial proposing 'refined knitwear which enables you to dress from morning to night'. This suggests a completely new way of dressing for the smart woman of the 1950s. Instead of a formal fitted suit for day and perhaps a full-length, strapless gown for evening, a one-step alternative is suggested in knitwear in which multi-functionalism and refinement are combined. An example of this can be seen in figure 42, *Linea Maglia*'s 1956 recommendation 'for elegant occasions'. This Spagnoli cross top in azure blues, is decorated with a 'worked edge' and worn with plain Capri pants. In the same year there is an article featuring city dresses and suits in jersey wool for the first time.

Figure 35. Krizia jumpsuit in dog-tooth check, worn with a sleeveless mohair
jerkin. Source: *Bellezza*, July 1959, p. 115.

Of the city dresses featured in autumn 1956, the Veneziani Sport model
(figure 43) was especially elegant, yet relatively unrestrictive. A simple
mustard dress with a stand-up collar, belted waist and three-quarter sleeves,
it was designed by a couturier for ready-to-wear production. Also illustrated
were high-quality ready-to-wear city suits by Avolio and Wanda. All are
loosely fitted and simple in effect, yet with interesting detailing, such as
contrasting collar and cuffs, a Chinese-style collar and check fabric jacket
edging to match the skirt. Although the feature was shot in monochrome,
the colours 'strawberry pink', 'green and maroon stripes' are stressed and
are clearly a selling point. These examples indicate that the properties of
knitwear, previously used predominantly outside fashion for practicality and
warmth, now offered the key stylistic elements noted in Italian fashion success.
Moreover, it reflected changing lifestyles by bridging the gap between formal
and informal wear.

Figure 36. Brunelli ski-wear, comprising red blouson and black trousers. Source: *Linea Italiana*, Winter 1949, p. 14.

Coverage of Italian boutique clothes for women by the American press did not lag behind that of the Italian media, and forms a guide to the US perspective of Italian boutique style. *Women's Wear Daily* drew attention to boutique as early as 1951, the year of the first collective Italian presentations. Indeed in the subsequent fifteen years, Italian boutique fashion is generally mentioned with greater enthusiasm than the couture in *WWD*.[32] The reports again place particular stress on the levels of innovation and use of fabric in boutique. In August 1951, for example, a report entitled 'Inventive Italian Boutique Items', accompanied by a full page of illustrations, described 'the inventiveness of design and fabric excitement'. It explained that each garment was 'a success in the boutique featuring it', and recommended that 'all could be peaked for main floor merchandising'. Examples included smock and slacks by Pucci, gloved scarf by Antonelli, embroidered velvet jacket by Bertoli, corded tiered skirt by Visconti, raincoat by Veneziani and long gloves by Fontana. The issues raised in this report were echoed a few months later,

Figure 37. Veneziani, Moro, Lilian and Rina beachwear on the quayside: afternoon
dresses, playsuits, smocks, capri pants, wraps, bikinis, and hooded
tops. Source: *Linea Italiana*, Summer 1949, p. 9.

with the headline 'Sports Fashion Originality, Fabric Appeal, Highlights of
First Italian Showings'. This article explained that 'fabrics play a big role in
the fashion interest of these showings', and mentioned jolly colour combinations, prints, and embroideries, as well as practical outdoor garments such
as pedal pushers and swimsuits. It is precisely this combination which holds
the key to the international success of Italian boutique in the 1950s and
early 1960s.

The casual nature of the boutique is stressed increasingly in *WWD*. In
July 1952, it reported that 'Sportswear exemplifies the flair for the casual',
and there are any number of examples of such descriptions of Italian boutique
by *WWD* in the 1950s. In January 1955, for example, 'novelties for every
kind of sportswear' were announced, followed by 'striped terry cloth beachwear', 'separates by Emilio Pucci which stress the traditional Italian colourings
of bright hues against solid black', and 'shorts and little sweaters by Mirsa'.
By January 1957, when a 'US Record on Sportswear Buying in Italy' was
noted, the key facets of Italian boutique were said to be 'outstanding prints'
and an 'offbeat but wearable style'.

Figure 38. Striped one-piece playsuit by Mirsa, with elasticated waist. Source: *Linea Maglia*, Spring 1956, p. 35.

At the beginning of the 1960s, Emilio Pucci was interviewed by *WWD* about the future of Italian fashion, and offered his perception of Italian style, under the revealing headline, 'Pucci Sees Couture Doom, Ties High Fashion to Ready-to-Wear'. The journalist stated that 'Mr Pucci has a very definite idea of what the immediate future cycle will be: an increasing trend towards the casual look'. Pucci defined this, saying 'casual to me means a woman who perfectly co-ordinates her clothes but still gives the air of great nonchalance'. The implication in all of these US press reports is that the essence of Italian boutique style rested not only on fresh simplicity, but also on the appearance of indifference created with the utmost care.

Figure 39. Greider ski-wear, comprising yellow jumper, yellow and orange knitted hat, black gloves and ski-trousers. Source: *Linea Maglia*, Winter 1954, p. 29.

The difference between the Italian design attitude by the early 1960s and that associated with Paris is captured by Elisa Massai, writing for *WWD* in July 1962: 'The French base design on formal, elaborate indoor parties, the Italians stress the carefree outdoor life, against a backdrop of nature. For the gala evenings, the "important" dress must come from Paris, for the unconventional parties one should wear Italian clothes'. The association of Italian fashion with the carefree and the casual seems to have been one of the greatest attractions for the US market. Massai's role in promoting Italian fashion in the US from 1948 was immense, because she was an Italian, and because she recognised how and why the US was so crucial to the Italian fashion industry.

Although US *Vogue* offers a more select perspective of US attitudes to Italian fashion, the magazine's stress was placed on the casual from the start. One of the earliest reports of Italian fashion was 'The Fine Italian Hand', by

Figure 40. Veneziani-Sport unfitted chamois leather jacket. Source: *Linea Italiana*, Autumn 1951, p. 110.

Marya Mannes, published in September 1946. Even at this early date, fabrics, colours, prints and a relaxed look were noted: 'the beauty of Italian silks', 'Italian women dote on prints . . . plain colours simply do not look well against the hot walls of Italian cities', 'the air is a casual one, played down rather than played up'. In September 1951, *Vogue* published an article entitled 'From the Italian Collections, Casual Clothes', following the second Florentine presentations in July that year. It was stated that although 'the couture collections are disappointing, the Sport and Boutique collections are excellent'. Veneziani Sport in particular 'created a sensation', with colours, sweaters, and cord jackets. Pucci and Simonetta boutique were also praised, and 'almost everyone bought'.

Two months later, in November 1951, US *Vogue* equated Italian style to outdoor casuals even more firmly, with the headline 'Resort Fashions – the Italian Look'. Under the sub-heading 'Italian Ideas for any South', the article recommended Italian boutique design, such as that by Pucci, for its 'fabrics of great variety and beauty, colours unconventional and full of character,

Figure 41. Emilio Pucci's printed 'fishtail' cotton Capri pants and thong sandals, worn with a fisherman-style jumper and set against a backdrop of boats and fishermen. Source: *Linea Maglia*, Summer 1954, pp. 42–7.

and original taste'. Also given were details of where and how to obtain the clothes in the US. The descriptions imply that Italian style was suitable for any holiday destination or warm climate, including America's West Coast, and the hot summers of the East Coast. *Vogue*'s interest in Italian boutique continued through the 1950s, and remained centred on casual items such as 'The Summer Sweater', or 'Italian Sunshoes, Pants and Sweaters'.

In 1960, even French *Vogue* devoted six pages to 'Shopping en Italie', its first acknowledgement of Italian fashion. Not surprisingly, the French ignored Italian couture in favour of 'Italian buys which say happy holidays'. Boutique sportswear by Simonetta, Pucci, Mirsa and Galitzine, such as silk trouser suits with slim, cropped legs, is presented through touristic images and well-known modern Italian products, such as Vespa scooters parked by the Tiber in Rome. Presumably, the French felt that such clothes posed little threat to their own bastion of high fashion.

Figure 42. Spagnoli cardigan 'for elegant occasions', with lace-effect bodice, and a Spagnoli cross top in azure blues, decorated with a 'worked edge' and worn with plain capri pants. Source: *Linea Maglia*, Summer 1954, p. 55.

It is clear that Italian boutique design was seen by US and the domestic press to be stylistically different from Italian couture right from its inception in the immediate post-war years, in terms of both its informality and moderate surface decoration, and this is substantiated by analysis of the few surviving garments. Boutique design was also seen to be especially different from French fashion which was associated with the formal, and was recognised for ease, colour, fabric and innovation, if not unorthodoxy. The media coverage shows that from the immediate post-war years the boutique collections were seen to be the most stylistically interesting category of Italian fashion production, and with hindsight it is evident that they were the most directional.

Italian Ready-to-wear Style 1951–1965

The stylistic evolution of Italian ready-to-wear is much more difficult to pin-point than that of couture or boutique. This is because press coverage was so limited, even in Italian magazines, until the mid-1960s. Therefore the evidence

Figure 43. Ready-to-wear 'city' dress and suit in jersey wool: a Veneziani Sport simple mustard dress with a stand-up collar, belted waist and three-quarter sleeves and boxy suits by Avolio and Wanda. All are loosely fitted and simple in effect, yet with interesting detailing. Source: *Linea Maglia*, Autumn 1956, pp. 12–24.

for this section is in the form of a case study of one of the leaders of the development of Italian ready-to-wear, MaxMara, founded in 1951. The information for this case study comes predominantly from an interview with the founder Achille Maramotti, as well as the contents of the MaxMara archive.[33]

MaxMara products were confined to coats and suits until the mid-1960s and were aimed predominantly at the upper middle class. There was little contact between the embryonic clothing industries of Europe when MaxMara was established in 1951, so it was probably inevitable that its founder Achille Maramotti looked to America for his initial stylistic inspiration. He perused a copy of *Harper's Bazaar*, which was available in Italy in the bigger towns and by mail order, and was very interested by advertisements for American ready-to-wear companies. The first MaxMara coat was a copy of one advertised

Figure 44. MaxMara suit with belted pocket detail, 1956. Source: MaxMara archive, Reggio Emilia, photographic records. Courtesy of MaxMara SRL.

in *Harper*'s by 'Lilli-Anne' of San Francisco. It was a bell-shape cut all in one with kimono sleeves. The suit was one of a series of garments awarded a medal for 'exquisite design and superb styling, lovely fabric, fine tailoring, smooth elegance . . . the custom-made look' and was available at 'fine stores' for 'about ninety dollars'. This description of the Lilli-Anne product could also have been used to describe Maramotti's intentions for the MaxMara style and the MaxMara market.

An example of MaxMara's style in the mid-1950s is seen in figure 44, a relatively simple tailored suit, photographed with a copy of *Vogue* for high fashion kudos. Between about 1956 and 1963 the company took its lead directly from French fashion, and Maramotti went to Paris twice-yearly to see the haute couture collections, and to buy toiles.[34] Typically, he would buy two or three coat and suit designs from each of Dior, Balenciaga, Givenchy and Balmain. Designs were then 'translated' for ready-to-wear production. Balenciaga's approach was seen as being closest to the MaxMara attitude and his designs were preferred for their easily translatable clean lines and strict proportions, whilst the exaggerated styles of the House of Dior had to

Figure 45. Four versions of 'Base 11', drawn by Gianni Iotti for MaxMara in 1962. Source: MaxMara archive, Reggio Emilia, photographic records. Courtesy of MaxMara SRL.

be more carefully 'reduced for industry'. Examples of this 'translation' process are seen in figure 45, which shows four versions of 'Base 11', drawn by Gianni Iotti for MaxMara.

Although this process was the norm in the UK and the US, it was not the norm in Italian ready-to-wear. Maramotti insists that he was the only Italian ready-to-wear representative who attended the Paris shows. In the early days at least, MaxMara's competitors were operating at a lower price level, and it would not have been financially viable for them, especially if they had to pay the full trade price. However, analysis of contemporary media indicates that these companies took inspiration from the international and domestic fashion press as they reported the Paris collections. There is therefore no evidence that the Italian ready-to-wear industry was following the Italian catwalks in the 1950s and early 1960s.[35]

Conclusion

This chapter has demonstrated that there was an internationally recognised Italian style at couture, boutique and ready-to-wear levels by 1965. The contemporary press coverage shows that the international fashion business had a very clear commercial understanding of the national style differences in fashion in the 1945–65 period. Initially, foreign buyers were attracted to Italian fashion for the combination of French-led style and low-prices at couture level. They were pleased with the high technical and aesthetic quality of Italian couture, in relation to the prices, particularly its fabrics, and the hand-sewn decoration, which was highly sophisticated. Increasingly, simple lines and effective use of colour were also noted. Although the buyers came at first to see the couture, even in the 1940s, the casual yet elegant nature of Italian boutique style was highly praised. Boutique was seen to fit the mood of the times, and offered something very different to French couture, whilst developing the Italian reputation for quality, fabric and colour. By the mid-1960s, this casually elegant look was also emerging at ready-to-wear level.

The significance of these points is confirmed by a US *Vogue* report of September 1952: 'There are three exciting things about Italian fashion today: the first is in the fact that Italy is capable of producing a kind of clothes which suit America exactly – and producing them in a manner unequalled by any other European country. Namely, clothes for outdoors, for resorts, for travel, for skiing; separates, fads, looks, airs, tricks – all the gay things, all the boutique articles and accessories. The second is the fabrics – anything and everything pertaining to Italian fabrics is newsworthy. The third is the evening dresses, marvellously made in marvellous silks at a relatively low cost. These are the three things in which the Italians need to be encouraged; they should be given wings to develop their native specialists and urgently discouraged from French adaptations – a tendency fast becoming a trend, and only because it is hoped that this will attract the American buying public.'[36] This report shows that right from the early 1950s, these characteristics were not only recognised by the American fashion industry, they were seen to be ideally suited to, and directed at, the American market. Moreover, the implication is that the success of Italian fashion lay in the hands of Americans.

Notes

1. Pitti Palace, Florence, GMA 50. This gown was made in Naples, c. 1889–90.
2. Maria Pezzi in interview, Milan, 13.10.95. Pezzi recounts how, for example, the 'Villa' agency negotiated a contract with Chanel, to reproduce the French fabric used in the original model, with an Italian fabric house; the exclusive trimmings and fastenings were provided directly by the couture house.
3. For further details of the inter-war development of fashion in Italy, see Butazzi, Grazietta, *1922–1943 Vent'Anni di Moda Italiana*, Centro Di, Florence, 1980.

4. Ibid.

5. Dior's 'New Look' (Corolla Line) and the resurgence of Paris haute couture after the War is well documented. The most recent assessment is *The New Look: the Dior Revolution*, Cawthorne, Nigel, Hamlyn, London, 1996. For its reception in America see De Petri, Stephen, and Leventon, Melissa, *New Look to Now: French Haute Couture 1947–1987*, Rizzoli, New York, 1989.

6. Ballard, Bettina, *In my Fashion*, Secker and Warburg, London, 1960, p. 184.

7. Steele, Valerie, 'Italian Fashion and America', in Celant, Germano, (ed.), *Italian Metamorphosis 1943–68*, Guggenheim, New York, 1994, p. 497.

8. *Les Femmes D'Aujourd'hui*, 3 April 1955.

9. See Steele, Valerie, *Paris Fashion: a Cultural History*, Oxford University Press, New York, 1988.

10. This issue was examined by the author in an unpublished undergraduate thesis entitled 'The Commercialisation of the Paris Haute Couture Industry 1947–1965', University of Brighton, 1986.

11. *Italian Metamorphosis 1943–68*, Guggenheim, New York, 1994. 530, from the private collection of Giancarlo Calza, Milan, and 531, from the Umberto Tirelli private collection, Rome.

12. Pitti Palace dress collection, TA 3898/9, label reads 'Irene Galitzine Roma'; Victoria and Albert Museum collection, T220-74, and T220A, label reads 'Irene Galitzine Roma', dated c.1962. It was unusual to find trousers in contemporary French haute couture collections.

13. M. H. De Young Memorial Museum, 1991.83.2a-b, label reads 'Ferrario Milano'. Spaghetti straps are knotted and dropped inside the dress which indicates that the dress was worn strapless at least sometimes. An American-made underwired strapless bra was added to the bodice by the original owner.

14. Melissa Leventon, Curator of Costume, in interview at the M. H. De Young Memorial Museum, San Francisco, 22.8.94. See also M. H. De Young Memorial Museum, 1991.83.1, 1950 Ferrario full-length silk evening gown embroidered with black sequins, worn by Naz Mardikian.

15. M. H. De Young Memorial Museum, 1993.16.6. Label reads 'Simonetta Roma'.

16. Leventon interview, San Francisco, 22.8.94.

17. Mrs Rosekrans has also donated a number of later garments by Japanese designer Issey Miyake who is known for his 'alternative style'.

18. V&A, T323-78. Label reads 'Fabiani Roma'.

19. V&A, T170.74. No label.

20. V&A, T322.78. Label reads 'Fabiani Roma'.

21. Settembrini, Luigi, 'From Haute Couture to Prêt-à-Porter', in Celant, Germano, *Italian Metamorphosis*, Guggenheim, New York, 1994, p. 485.

22. Strini interview, near Florence, 18.10.95.

23. Ballard, Bettina, *In My Fashion*, Secker and Warburg, London, 1960, p. 254.

24. Museum of the City of New York, 86.25.11 bodysuit dated late 1940s, 86.25.12 blouse, late 1940s, 86.25.15 blouse 1950s, 72.100.6 skirt 1950s, 72.194.2

dress early 1960s, 72.194.3a-e pant-suit early 1960s, 73.133.3 tunic 1965, 73.133.4 shirt 1965. Simonetta and Fabiani evening dress 1950s, and 93.6.2 Galitzine evening dress mid-1960s, 77.98.42.

25. This compares to (1950s) 9 Fabiani, 1 Fontana and 1 Gattinoni; (1960s) 3 Bertoli, 2 Capucci, 7 Fabiani, 3 Fontana, 2 Galitzine, 4 Missoni, and 14 Valentino. US museums typically hold far more garments by Pucci than by any other Italian designer.

26. V&A, T310 +1. Label reads 'Simonetta Sport Roma. Made in Italy'.

27. This method was pioneered by Italian-born couturier Elsa Schiaparelli, who worked in Paris in the inter-war period.

28. Included in 'La Sala Bianca: Nascita della Moda Italiana' (video), VideoCast, Florence, 1992.

29. *Linea Italiana*, Spring 1956, p. 35.

30. *Linea Italiana*, Spring 1951, p. 42.

31. *Linea Italiana*, Autumn 1951, p. 56.

32. In the early 1950s, the term 'boutique' (or sportswear) used in *WWD*, equated to garments by designers of high-quality, fashionable, ready-to-wear clothes, such as Pucci, and accessories by couturiers such as Fontana, and had not yet broadened to include boutique lines by couturiers. By the late 1950s boutique (or sportswear, or resortwear) had come to mean very high-quality, ready-to-wear garments presented at the Florentine collections and designed by either couturiers or boutique designers, as well as high-quality casual clothing by manufacturers, usually known as 'sportswear houses'. The term ready-to-wear was used only occasionally, because of the persistent low-quality reputation of ready-to-wear, especially in Europe.

33. Maramotti interview, Reggio Emilia, 21.7.95. Also, Laura Lusuardi, employee of MaxMara since the early 1950s, in interview at the MaxMara factory in Reggio Emilia, 19.7.95. Lusuardi is now Fashion Co-Ordinator at MaxMara.

34. According to journalist and illustrator, Maria Pezzi (in interview, Milan, 13.10.95), an old acquaintance who also went to the collections, Maramotti bought as a private client, and did not pay the full trade price, which was very high. MaxMara's target market was broad; any shape and any age could wear a loosely fitting coat, or a semi-fitted suit. Nonetheless, within this, Maramotti states that 'the "typical" customer was the provincial doctor's wife', or in other words, the wives of the professional classes. Later this developed into the woman who works and is a target in her own right, rather than one who is defined in terms of her husband's position and income.

35. However, in approximately 1964, Maramotti stopped going to the Paris collections to buy. In the later 1960s, the numbers of trade buyers in Paris began to decline and the traditional subservience to French haute couture waned. Significantly, Maramotti was one of the earliest manufacturers to take this plunge. See the unpublished BA (Hons) thesis by the author, entitled 'The Commercialisation of the Paris Haute Couture Industry 1947–1965', University of Brighton, 1986.

36. US *Vogue*, 5.9.52, page unknown, 'Italian Collection Notebook'.

4

The Relationship between America and Italian Style

This chapter establishes the significance of current research into America's cultural importance in post-war Europe and evaluates the significance of the little-known relationship between American culture and the Italian fashion industry. This study has shown that many of the preconditions for Italian economic growth in the post-war years were established with the assistance of the US government, largely through Marshall Aid and industrial co-operation between the two countries. Such political and economic power formed a framework for the export of American culture to Italy.

The Significance of US Cultural Models in Italy

The way in which culture relates to the political and economic structure of a nation has been the subject of much recent theoretical debate. Most contemporary commentators agree that although culture represents broad tendencies within political economies, to some extent, culture also has its own autonomy, or 'national identity'. In the early part of this century, Antonio Gramsci addressed this issue and developed the concept of hegemony to describe the role of culture in relation to power.[1] Whilst Gramsci was more concerned with the position of social classes within nations, his concept may also be used to analyse the significance of intellectual and material cultures in the power which one nation may have over another. Thus, the cultural relationship between the US and Italy is an important context to the stylistic development of Italian fashion, and its affinity to American style.

Although modern structures of capitalist production were in place in Italy by the 1930s, the development of mass audiences and markets was an uneven process, and was not complete until well after the Second World War.[2] Indeed it was only in the 1950s and early 1960s that Italy moved from a predominantly rural society to consumer capitalism. Not only did real incomes rise in Italy's post-war economic boom, providing large numbers of people with some disposable money, but the proportion of skilled and white-collar workers expanded, and the population became increasingly urbanised. The Italian people were aware of consumer goods, and were keen to acquire them. Furthermore, consumer goods were firmly associated in the public mind with the United States of America. The relationship between America and the famous aesthetic of Italian post-war industrial design is pertinent to this and has been analysed in some detail by Penny Sparke in recent years.[3] Sparke questions whether Italy's post-war international reputation for highly innovative, modern design objects, was dependent on the pre-existing US model. It is clear that at least one major facet of Italian industry was inspired by American (Fordist) manufacturing processes.

American industrial design emerged in the inter-war period, as a method of injecting desirability into consumer products.[4] The famous designer Walter Dorwin Teague played a significant part within the movement and in 1950 travelled to Italy to select objects for a touring exhibition in the US entitled, 'Italy at Work'. He chose a range of products from traditional craft to industrially manufactured furniture in the modern style and in modern materials, as well as mass-produced engineered goods, such as the Lambretta Scooter (launched in 1946). Interestingly, Teague's trip was reported in the US by Fairchild Publications in May 1950, under the title 'Jury chooses Italian Ceramics for Brooklyn Museum Exhibit'. The exhibition was intended to develop trade links between the two countries. Its impact was two-fold. Firstly, as Fairchild noted, it 'convinced the experts that Italian artisans, if properly directed, can reduce their prices and cater successfully to American tastes'. Secondly, as Penny Sparke points out, it helped to establish the character of Italian design. Moreover, it affected both the Italian approach to the American market, and the way the American market perceived Italian design.

Sparke explains that 'while one face of Italian industry looked to America for help and inspiration in the area of Fordist mass manufacture, another, chiefly the smaller factories and workshops, was content to follow a more traditional trajectory'.[5] This was precisely the same pattern as that seen in the Italian fashion industry. Italian industrial products were increasingly redolent of the American aesthetic of 'streamlining', and the new generation of Italian designers, such as Gio Ponti, took up the idiom wholeheartedly.[6] The international reputation of these designers as arbiters of style can only have been a beneficial association for the Italian fashion industry. As levels of consumption rose dramatically in the late 1950s, a new profession of independent designers (such as Ettore Sottsass) became famous for their role in encouraging consumers to buy such goods, in much the same way as Teague and his compatriots had done in the interwar years.[7]

However, it is now clear that while the US exerted a strong influence on Italian design in this period, Italy also developed design and manufacturing ideas independently from the US, ideas which were rooted in native traditions and approaches. In general, Italian products were imbued with high-quality, cosmopolitan connotations. The key disparity can be identified in the continued Italian dependence on historic traditions which survived alongside the expansion of mass production. This links many Italian goods to 'high culture', rather than 'popular culture', while most American products belonged firmly in the latter category. Furthermore, although large-scale mass-production expanded in Italy in these years, a parallel network of small-scale, craft-based industries continued to play a crucially important role in both the image of Italian products, and the Italian economy. Sparke concludes that this combination of 'small-scale manufacture with a progressive attitude to manufacture and product appearance marked the country out on the international design map in the post-war years'.[8]

Sparke's reading has important connotations for the evolution of the Italian fashion industry, because it is possible to draw comparisons between the relationship of Italian industrial design to America, and that between the Italian fashion industry and America. Whilst Italian fashion enjoyed an increasingly high profile in terms of its innovative design, it cannot be said to have been the subject of intense contemporary debate. Nor can rational comparisons be drawn between the Italian industrial design aesthetic and that of the Italian fashion industry. However, it is evident that the development of the industry was inspired by American (Fordist) manufacturing processes. Furthermore, although Italian fashion style drew upon the modern notion of casual sportswear, which was the US forté, it developed the look on the basis of native traditions and approaches, enhanced by an injection of fresh contemporaneity.

The significance of another aspect of US culture, the movie industry, to Italian culture, and more specifically to Italian fashion, is also crucial here. The cultural modernisation of Europe, and America's role within it, is often referred to as 'Americanisation'. This process has received considerable attention, both by contemporary commentators amongst the intellectual elite, and modern scholars, especially in the last decade.[9] In 1955, Reuters published the results of a small survey entitled 'Is the Free World Being Americanised?'. The report concluded that Italy was not being Americanised to any significant degree. Some impact was noted amongst urban youth, but in the rural areas little impact was noted at all. For many years, these results were seen as hard evidence of the strength of European national identities. However, it is now apparent that American customs were widely adopted, especially amongst the young, although there were different patterns in different European countries. In 1992, Italian historian David Ellwood re-assessed the Reuters' findings, in *Rebuilding Western Europe: America and Post-War Reconstruc-*

tion, and established that by the mid-1950s the Americanisation of Europe was an acknowledged process.

As early as 1943, US soldiers who were in Italy for the Liberation offered a cultural bridge between the two countries. They sold American goods such as T-shirts, jeans and nylons on the black market, and brought a taste of American consumerism for those who could afford it. According to journalist Elisa Massai, 'mutual sympathy' between the two countries was encouraged by the fact that so many GI's were from Italian immigrant families, and spoke some form of Italian.[10] Certainly, it is felt by most historians that whilst the British remembered that it was they (unlike the Americans) who had been at war with Italy, the American soldiers, fighting in Italy from 1943, became more deeply involved in Italian life, and many found a partner there; this relationship has been described as 'a mass discovery of Italy by the Americans originally sent there against their will'.[11] The post-war programmes of economic and military aid sent hundreds of American experts to Italy, especially economists, agriculturalists and naval men, and the 'discovery' of Italy by Americans increased the momentum.

From 1947, rich Americans began to visit Italy as tourists in growing numbers, encouraged by Italy's inexpensive cost of living, cultural heritage and reliable sunshine, and easier cross-Atlantic travel. In this year, for example, *Life* explained to its readers that 'In the fancy restaurants of Rome and Milan anyone with 1,500 lire can make a gourmet's selection from tables swamped with delicacies. To an American this price is only 2.50 dollars.' According to *WWD*, by 1950 'The first tourists had returned to Venice, Capri and the Riviera and bought sandals, hats and Emilio [Pucci] clothes. Holy year, 1950, attracted thousands of tourists to Rome.' In 1951, US *Vogue* described 'cheap petrol, uncrowded highways, glory and glamour, modern transport, good hotels, delicious food, fascinating shops', and of course, 'full value for your dollar'. Americans were further seduced by images of Italy in quality American magazines. In March 1954, for example, the Italian State Tourist Office (ENIT) placed an advertisement in *Vogue* which invited the wealthy American to 'see Italy first', 'for all that makes a perfect holiday'. Under a photograph of a Venetian gondola, 'exciting offerings in world-famous shops', 'pageantry, history, color, art and music' are mentioned, and again, 'on the practical side', the 'excellent dollar values'. From the early 1950s, American films shot in Italy contributed to the American idea of Italy as a quaint and fascinating paradise. Shot in the most photogenic locations, hits such as *Roman Holiday* (1953) purveyed an enchanting, if sentimental image of Italy, and represented a free and effective publicity campaign for Italian tourism.

Official US propaganda in Europe in this period was not restricted to promotion of the Marshall Plan, as Ellwood has explained: 'By pointing to the most credible, alluring way forward from recovery to modernisation in a hundred different ways – personalities, products, magazines, advertising, films, television, fashions, lifestyles – this kind of influence was turned into Americanisation'.[12] Ellwood thus concluded that the US government deliberately engineered the dissemination of American customs into virtually every aspect of Italian life, for all social classes, in an effort to encourage higher levels of capitalist mass consumption, through changes in behaviour and mentality.

In the light of this it seems sensible to consider whether American fashion style had a significant relationship with Italian fashion style. Recent publications concerning the cultural relationship between the two nations offer a relevant framework in which stylistic identities can be related. Stephen Gundle's 1996 article, which addresses the Americanisation of Italian daily life in the 1950s, offers an incisive analysis of the scale and impact of 'Americanisation' in relation to the rise of mass-consumption in Italy.[13] In addition, David Forgacs' *Culture in the Industrial Era 1880–1980: Cultural Industries, Politics and the Public*, offers a detailed analysis in which the interplay between Italy and the US is seen as a key facet of the cultural modernisation process.[14]

Both Gundle and Forgacs propose that Italy was probably the most receptive European country to American cultural input in the 1950s. Forgacs attributes this to Italy's late unification, which meant that 'Italian national culture was traditionally difficult to maintain'. Of particular importance is the fact that Gundle and Forgacs focus on the development of cultural industries, such as film. Through analysis of consumption, they conclude that the Italian reception of the American model is the critical factor. Gundle specifically refutes the notion that American influence can be seen purely as 'cultural imperialism', previously proposed by authors such as Herbert Schiller, and states that 'although the American desire to exploit new demands and markets was strong, Americanisation was not imposed'.[15]

Although the precise role of the US in Italy's cultural modernisation remains difficult to pinpoint, Forgacs concludes that whilst exogenous factors (such as Hollywood's search for export markets), endogenous factors (such as Italian exhibitor demand for popular films) and political factors (such as inadequate Italian import controls) were important, attitudinal factors (such as changes in public taste) were the most decisive. Describing the strength of European desire for American products as a 'yearning', Gundle is clear that in the 1950s, the United States was seen as a model to aspire to, and determines that although Catholic forces were able to limit some changes, 'if a global overview is taken, it is indisputable that the general trend has been one of diffuse acceptance'.

After the liberation of Italy, an aggressive dumping of Hollywood films began, and for a long period after the War, Italy continued to be the greatest importer of films from the US to Europe. The fascist Monopoly Law was repealed in 1945, under pressure from the Americans, and most Hollywood studios opened or re-opened Italian branches. In the first year, the US sent over 600 films.[16] The market relations of this issue were addressed by Christopher Wagstaff in a recent paper entitled 'Italy in the Post-War International Cinema Market'.[17] Wagstaff explains that the US government and the US film industry worked hard to re-establish American films in the Italian market, and the Italian authorities acquiesced. Six years of unseen films were offloaded, together with new releases through a block booking system, which obliged exhibitors to take two extra films with every film they had chosen. The innovative neo-realist films for which Italy is so well known, were in reality only a small proportion of films seen there. At the same time, Italy became an increasingly important market for Hollywood, as tickets sold doubled from 411 million in 1946, to 819 million in 1955.[18] These figures reflect popular taste as well as the desires of American and Italian distributors.

Moreover, Hollywood was facing declining domestic audiences and sought to cut costs. Decentralisation of some production to Italy, especially Rome, was seen as a viable method, because of cheap wages and studio rentals, the high technical quality of Italian personnel and US tax advantages for investing abroad until 1968. US stars came to Italy to make films and with them came Hollywood glamour. Whilst Italians had seen the Hollywood lifestyle in American films before the War, it was now to be found in Italy. Beverley Hills-style houses and cars appeared, and resorts such as Portofino became internationally famous. The impact of this industry, dubbed 'Hollywood on the Tiber', is encapsulated in Federico Fellini's famous 1959 film *La Dolce vita* (the Sweet Life). Perhaps the most significant moment is when the character of the glamorous America star, played by Anita Ekberg, arrives triumphantly at Rome airport, surrounded by 'paparazzi' and flowers, as the embodiment of the American myth. Furthermore, US stars dominated the Italian box office. The new generation of international Italian stars, such as Gina Lollobrigida, were referred to as *bellezze americane* (beautiful American-style women), and individuals were often likened to particular Hollywood stars. Even Silvana Mangano, who presented a natural and earthy image at odds with the glamour of Hollywood, was described as 'the Rita Hayworth of the Italian periphery'.

Italian films in this period reflect Italy's postwar social and cultural transition. One example is *Riso amaro* (Bitter Rice) of 1948, in which the heroine played by Silvana Mangano looks like both Rita Hayworth and Jane Russell, is addicted to American music, film and fashion, dances the boogie-woogie and chews gum, a habit which encapsulated American behaviour in popular culture. In a later film *Un Americano a Roma* (An American in Rome) of 1953, the central character parodies these cultural changes by rejecting the traditional Italian lifestyle, and living a fantasised Hollywood existence in jeans and T-shirts. Clearly, the cinema both reflected cultural transition and played an active part in the change. On one hand, as Gundle explains, 'The cinema was itself an agent of social change, in a country in transition from an agricultural to an industrial economy; it was an educator, a source of new ideas'. On the other hand, as David Ellwood and Rob Kroes have demonstrated, America's cinema 'had moved into the collective life of the Italian people and had changed their ways of dressing, speaking, walking, amusing themselves – projecting itself, above all, as the magic mirror of their future prosperity, full employment, democracy and happiness.'[19]

However, the most significant shift in cultural consumption, in terms of audience size, was television. Mass audience preceded mass ownership; in 1958, for example, one million licences were sold but the viewing figure was estimated at over ten million. Like Hollywood, television proposed a prosperous vision of modern life. The first Italian television programmes were broadcast in 1954, early in Italy's economic expansion and industrial transformation. Sports, variety, musical entertainment, plays and quiz shows dominated the broadcasts. Quiz shows made the most conscious effort to imitate US television, and such programmes have been described as national events.

As a child in the 1950s, Italian fashion PR Luigi Settembrini recalls watching a variety of US programmes on Italian television, including the famous *Lascia o Raddoppia?*, which he says 'encapsulated the American lifestyle, and glorified mass consumption'. Based on the US programme Double or Quits, *Lascia o Raddoppia?* was hosted by an Italo-American called Mike Bongiorno, known as the 'Voice of America'. Settembrini explains that the programme was also shown in cinemas and in bars, so even those without a television set watched it avidly. Such programmes were in a position to affect a significantly high proportion of the Italian population. Despite intellectual criticism of the television as vulgar mass entertainment, by the late 1950s it became impossible to keep Italian culture 'Italian'. Italy was particularly susceptible to Americanisation in the 1950s due to three factors, as Gundle has shown: the lack of industrial basis, the velocity of the change which produced a demand for new suggestions, and the absence of a national culture which weakened possible filters to American input.[20]

The reasons why the Italian fashion industry assimilated American style differ slightly. Firstly, the entire Italian populace, including fashion designers and manufacturers, had an awareness of American fashion style, or at least what they thought was American style. Secondly, at the outset, in the early

1950s, as this study has shown, Italian fashion output was directed predominantly at the American market, and therefore much design was moulded to American tastes. Thirdly, Hollywood film stars, international icons of style and beauty, formed an important market for Italian high fashion in the 1951–65 period, and Italian designers were more than happy to cater for their specific tastes. The link between the US movie industry and Italian fashion was summed up aptly by *WWD* in June 1955 when it reported that 'Film making also gave a fillip to the fashion industries: American film stars and companies were beginning to make films in Rome, and discovering that Italian clothes were pretty and less expensive than those in New York or Paris.

The Relationship between Cinema and High Fashion

Recent research into the impact of Hollywood in Italy has not considered dimensions such as styles of dress in any depth, yet the relationship of Hollywood with Italian fashion had two important consequences. Firstly, American actresses, in Rome for the shooting of numerous films as part of 'Hollywood on the Tiber', patronised Roman couturiers for their private wardrobes from the late 1940s. Secondly, both Hollywood studios and Italian filmmakers employed these couturiers to create the film wardrobes for a number of films shot in Rome. The Fontana sisters, along with Schuberth, were the two Italian houses most frequently patronised by film stars. According to Gloria Bianchino, 'Fontana was known as the dressmaker of movie heroines, where one could see clothes sufficient to keep the whole American industry going for a year'.[21] This may be an exaggeration, but it is clear that Fontana's reputation was founded on the association, fuelled by widespread and highly valuable publicity. Thus, the relationship between film and Fontana offers an important case study here.

Sorelle Fontana's strong links with American stars were built up through 'Hollywood on the Tiber', from 1946 onwards, and there are a number of photographs in the Fontana archive, depicting famous Hollywood stars at the atelier, or wearing Fontana clothes. These include Myrna Loy, Loretta Young and Linda Christian, who all wore decorative evening dresses for 1948 publicity photographs in figure 46. However, according to Micol, Fontana's 'big break' came in 1949, when Linda Christian wore a Fontana gown for her marriage to Tyrone Power, while the couple were in Rome for the filming of *Prince of the Foxes* (see figure 47). Indeed, Micol Fontana proclaims that 'Linda Christian made the Sorelle Fontana'. Certainly, the repercussions were immense. Fontana goes as far as to say that the wedding was reported in 'every newspaper world-wide', and from that moment 'everybody knew about Fontana'. It is important to note that this was almost two years before the

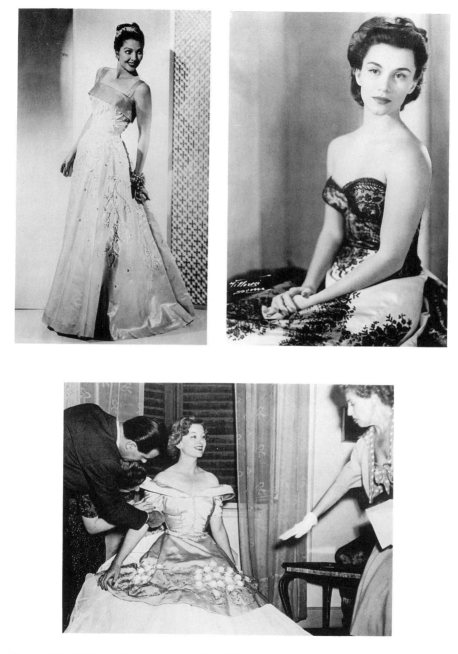

Figure 46. 1948 publicity photographs of Myrna Loy, Loretta Young and Linda
Christian wearing Fontana evening dress. Source: Fontana archive,
Rome, photographic records. Courtesy of Sorelle Fontana, Alta Moda
SRL.

Figure 47. Linda Christian at a fitting for her Fontana wedding gown, 1949. This garment is held in the Fontana archive, n.46/F Christian. Source: Fontana archive, Rome, photographic records. Courtesy of Sorelle Fontana, Alta Moda SRL.

first collective presentation of Italian high fashion to an international audience, organised by Giorgini in 1951.

In October 1951, Micol Fontana travelled to Hollywood as the guest and 'personal friend' of Christian and Power. During the trip Fontana presented what she describes as 'the first fashion show of Italian clothes in America' to Hollywood's stars. According to Fontana, Christian and Power organised the show for her, 'because they wanted all the movie stars to see Fontana clothes'. Fontana recalls that the room was very full and 'they all jumped on the runway afterwards, because it was new and different'; this is a specific claim for disparity from current Paris fashions, and for independent innovation. Fontana was also given a party in her honour at the Christian-Power Hollywood home and the memory of being whisked away in an American convertible by Cary Grant is still sharp. This was also the day that Christian and Power had their first child, and Fontana recalls taking her collection to Christian's maternity clinic, with Power, because she was unable to attend the show.

Such opportunities presented Sorelle Fontana with all the publicity they needed. From 1949 Fontana was photographed with the stars both in Hollywood and back in Rome, and was patronised by a gamut of names, including, for example: Myrna Loy (1949), in Rome filming *That Dangerous Age*, Grace Kelly (1949 and 1959) for evening dresses, Audrey Hepburn (1952) for her wedding dress, Merle Oberon (1952) for a cocktail dress, Ava Gardner (1953, 1954, 1956) for many items for her private wardrobe, Elizabeth Taylor (1954) for an evening dress, Kim Novak (1957) filming *The Sun also Rises*, Mrs Kirk Douglas (1961) during the filming of her husband in *The Indian Fighter*, and Jayne Mansfield for a bathing suit (1962).[22] Each visit was duly recorded for and by the press, as was the exhibition of Fontana clothes at social events. Linda Christian continued to be a loyal patron, and in October 1950, for example, was described by *Bellezza* as 'faithful to Sorelle Fontana,' choosing 'for the Venice Film Festival a black and green tulle cocktail dress'. Micol Fontana describes herself as the 'friend' of many of these stars, because, she says, 'when you dress people you become their friends; because you have to understand them inside'. Micol Fontana became godmother to Christian's second child, and surviving informal photographs of Fontana with both Christian and Gardner indicate that these two stars were certainly friends (see figure 48). Such friendships and such publicity can only have been fortuitous in business terms.

The Italian garments favoured by Hollywood stars for their private wardrobes fall predominantly into the evening wear category. Despite Micol Fontana's claim that the designs she presented in Hollywood were 'new and different', the evening gowns seen here broadly follow the current style set by Paris, with nipped-in waists, and either very full or narrow skirts, in what is often described as 'the nineteenth century style'. They are made of luxurious stuffs, such as velvet and silk satin, and almost all the designs involve considerable surface decoration. Although surface decoration was central to French evening wear in this period, it was a particular forté of the Italians as this study has shown, and was seen as Italy's 'traditional craft'. The stars' most popular form of surface decoration at Fontana, for example, was beaded embroidery and there is a striking similarity between such designs and the creations of many Hollywood costume designers. Indeed, the grand and

Figure 48. Informal photograph of Fontana shopping for souvenirs in Mexico with Ava Gardner, 1957. Source: Fontana archive, Rome, photographic records. Courtesy of Sorelle Fontana, Alta Moda SRL.

glittering Italian designs fitted neatly into the idea of American glamour expressed by Hollywood movies since the inter-war period.

Perhaps because it did not always have to conform to these ideas of glittering glamour, daywear can be seen as the most innovative area of Italian couture creation for Hollywood film stars. One of the best examples of this is the well-known black wool-silk 'cassock dress' designed for Ava Gardner by Sorelle Fontana in 1956 (figure 49). In its colour, fabric and style, the dress can be described as both striking and understated, but it caused quite a stir. In fact, the dress was part of Fontana's *Cardinale* collection for the

Figure 49. Fontana black wool-silk 'cassock dress' designed for Ava Gardner in 1956, part of the 'Cardinale collection'. Source: Fontana archive, Rome, photographic records. Courtesy of Sorelle Fontana, Alta Moda SRL.

autumn-winter season, but it was the combination of the clear religious reference (in a staunchly Catholic country), with a female Hollywood star known for her seductive beauty, which caused the stir (figure 50). With such publicity, the collection was assured commercial success. The dress was well enough known for it to be the obvious inspiration for Gherardi's 'cassock' design for Anita Ekberg in the famous dome scene in Fellini's *La Dolce Vita* a few years later.

The patronage of Hollywood stars encouraged the custom of other wealthy Americans, especially in the political arena. Margaret Truman and Jackie

Figure 50. Ava Gardner wearing the dress shown in figure 49. Source: Fontana archive, Rome, photographic records. Courtesy of Sorelle Fontana, Alta Moda SRL.

Kennedy were both Fontana clients. In 1953 Jackie Kennedy ordered an embroidered double-silk evening dress, and in 1956 Margaret Truman ordered her widely publicised wedding dress from Fontana (figure 51).[23] Few fashionable Americans could have remained unaware of Sorelle Fontana, and indeed, of Italian fashion, by the mid-1950s.

The new Italian stars of American cinema also patronised Italian fashion houses, but tended to favour Emilio Schuberth over the American stars' favourite, Sorelle Fontana. For example, both Gina Lollobrigida and Sofia Loren wore Schuberth's clothes at important social events, and were keen to

Figure 51. Margaret Truman in a Fontana wedding dress, 1956. This garment is held in the Fontana Archive, n.39/F Truman. Source: Fontana archive, Rome, photographic records. Courtesy of Sorelle Fontana, Alta Moda SRL.

advertise their link with him; the name of the couturier was always mentioned in press reports. One memorable example survives in the collection of the Pitti Palace Museum, an evening gown designed by Schuberth and worn by Lollobrigida in 1957 (figure 52). Part of Schuberth's *Solare* (solar) collection, the gown appears to reflect this through the hues created in nature by sunlight. From a dark moss-green at the waist, the delicately pleated silk chiffon tunic fades to cream at the bodice and hem, and is bounded by a wide band of cream silk grosgrain. The boned bodice was worn over a contrasting cream grosgrain fishtail skirt. The design is undecorated, but would have firmly

Figure 52. Schuberth two piece evening gown worn by Lollobrigida in 1957. Part of the 'Solare' (solar) collection. The delicately pleated silk chiffon tunic fades from a dark moss-green at the waist, to cream at the bodice and hem. The boned bodice was worn over a contrasting cream grosgrain fishtail skirt. Source: Pitti Palace, Florence, TA. 3891. Courtesy of the Ministero per i Beni e le Attività Culturali. Further reproductions or duplications by any means are forbidden.

drawn attention to Lollobrigida's renowned 22-inch waist. The use of colour and fabric, and the simplicity of the line fit snugly into the idea of Italy's developing fashion style. It should be noted that whilst Schuberth did not shun surface decoration in his designs, he preferred a less glittering form of embroidery than that typically favoured by Sorelle Fontana and seen in figure 53.

The loyalty of Italian stars to Schuberth can be seen in the contemporary press. Perhaps the best example of this is seen in the American magazine *Life*, which ran a cover feature entitled 'Gina Lollobrigida: a Star's Wardrobe', in January 1955. The cover photograph showed Lollobrigida in a relatively simple gown of figured satin, with no surface decoration, but a swathed cut which emphasised the star's celebrated physique. The magazine published 250 inch-high sketches of Lollobrigida's clothes, which she had drawn to save time identifying garments. It was reported that 'Lollobrigida's clothes

Figure 53. Jackie Kennedy in a Fontana evening gown with John F. Kennedy at a Washington Gala Ball, 1955. A typical example of Fontana's embroidery for evening wear. Source: Fontana archive, Rome, photographic records. Courtesy of Sorelle Fontana, Alta Moda SRL.

are all made in Italy, most of them by Rome's Emilio Schuberth, and are designed with an eye on Gina's figure, rather than on the season's new silhouettes.' This comment implies that the client, rather than Paris style, led Schuberth's design, an approach which can be compared to that of Hollywood's costume designers, who had worked this way since the inter-war period. The combination of Lollobrigida's generous custom and the American publicity she attracted, can only have been good business news for Schuberth. Hollywood stars, both Italian and (especially) American were evidently crucial to the early international success of Italian high fashion. However, their significance was not restricted to private patronage.

Roman couturiers also created film wardrobes for the stars. One of the earliest direct links between Italian high fashion and the cinema came in 1951, in an Italian film, when Roman couturier Antonelli designed the costumes for Matarazzo's *I figli di nessuno*, (Fatherless Children), a popular hit. Aware of the success of Italian designers, some Hollywood filmmakers seem to have used public interest in Roman couture as a way of attracting an audience for their films. One of the best examples of this is Mankiewitz's *The Barefoot Contessa* (La Contessa scalza) of 1954, an American production featuring a series of outfits by Fontana for Ava Gardner, which marked the start of the long collaboration between the star and the couture house. One of the grand evening gowns designed for the film is seen in figure 54. A bright blue confection of silk tulle and sequins, the gown was clearly intended to dazzle its audience.

One of the surviving costumes from the film is now at the Brooklyn Museum, a strapless pink evening gown with a full skirt, a fitted cape and very long open sleeves.[24] It is decorated with an embroidered bimorphic floral design in velvet and sequins, and has a distinct glamorous theatricality. Figure 55 is a contemporary publicity photograph showing both the gown and Micol Fontana. Sorelle Fontana also used this film to promote their name in other ways, such as asking Ava Gardner to model their forthcoming collection in Rome. According to Micol Fontana, this was 'big media news'. The media attention continued, and in 1957, for example, it was reported in *WWD* that Micol Fontana had 'accompanied Ava Gardner to Mexico, as the Fontanas are making her costumes for the film adaptation of Hemingway's novel, *The Sun Also Rises*.'

Another revealing detail of the relationship between Italian fashion and film is the representation of the fashion business on screen, by Italian film-makers.[25] One of the earliest instances of this is Antonioni's *Cronaca di un amore* (Story of a Love), of 1950, which includes scenes in a high fashion atelier, where the elegant heroine, a customer, gives a dress worth a mighty 300,000 Lire to one of the house models, reinforcing the glamour of haute couture in the eyes of the audience. Three years later, Emmer's *Le ragazze di Piazza di Spagna* (Three Girls from Rome), was shot at Sorelle Fontana's atelier, on the edge of the famous square. The film told the story of three girls, who worked as seamstresses, one of whom is promoted to the salon as a model. However, the story does not end as glamorously as Antonioni's, because the model's labourer boyfriend rebels and ultimately she chooses marriage over her job.

The film was seen in America, and was used as a publicity tool by Sorelle Fontana. An example of this can be seen in figure 56, a model photographed during the promotional tour, wearing a Fontana evening gown alongside a

Figure 54. Grand evening gown in sequinned blue tulle, designed for Ava Gardner in Mankiewitz's *The Barefoot Contessa*, (La Contessa Scalza) of 1954. Source: Fontana archive, Rome, original drawing. Courtesy of Sorelle Fontana, Alta Moda SRL.

board which invites Americans to 'Have lunch at the Zodiac, Friday at 1.00, and meet Madame Fontana and her three Italian models who will present her exciting couturier collection from the movie *Three Girls in Rome*, opening October 3, Captain Theatre'. Micol Fontana describes this trip as 'promoting Italian fashion', and recalls 'a warm welcome, with crowds applauding in the streets as we drove around in an open-top Alfa Romeo'. Clearly, it was not only important that Fontana was seen as part of Italian fashion, but also as an Italian, in an Italian car.

In her recently published memoirs, Micol Fontana reveals that she kept a diary of her visits to America, and felt more at home there than in Italy.[26] This may partly explain her affinity with American stars and American style. She also makes the crucial point that not only were her trips good for public relations, they were also 'to observe, study and compare people and their clothes'.[27] Fontana went to see what Americans wore, and what they wanted in their clothes.

Figure 55. Contemporary publicity photograph showing Micol Fontana with a strapless pink evening gown with a full skirt, a fitted cape and very long open sleeves, designed for Ava Gardner in Mankiewitz's *The Barefoot Contessa* (La Contessa Scalza), of 1954. The gown is decorated with an embroidered floral design in velvet and sequins. This garment is held at the Brooklyn Museum, 54205. Source: Fontana archive, Rome, photographic records. Courtesy of Sorelle Fontana, Alta Moda SRL.

Evidently, the links between cinema and Italian couture were very firm in the post-war years. The impact of these links was twofold. Firstly, Hollywood stars formed an important and probably essential market for Roman couturiers. It is unlikely that Roman couture as a whole, and particularly houses such as Fontana, would have achieved such international recognition and custom had it not been for the prestige imbued by names such as Ava Gardner. Although it must be noted that no such association existed for Florentine or Milanese couturiers, some of the Roman reputation must have rubbed off; all were 'Italian' to international eyes. Secondly, Fontana, and possibly other Italian couturiers tailored their designs to American tastes, not only of the stars themselves, but also of other wealthy women. Most Italians, including couturiers, were familiar with American culture and the styles of dress worn both in American films and by the stars who frequented

Figure 56. Model photographed during the US promotional tour for *Three Girls in Rome*, wearing a Fontana evening gown alongside a board which invites Americans to 'Have lunch at the Zodiac, Friday at 1.00, and meet Madame Fontana and her three Italian models who will present her exciting couturier collection from the movie opening October 3, Captain Theatre'. Source: Fontana archive, Rome, photographic records. Courtesy of Sorelle Fontana, Alta Moda SRL.

Rome in the immediate post-war years. Moreover, Fontana, at least, diligently investigated American requirements.

Identification of US Fashion Style and its Relationship to the Emerging Italian Style

Alongside a continuing allegiance to Paris fashion, there had always been a discernible simplicity in American attitudes to dress.[28] As early as 1928, American economist Paul Nystrom wrote that 'In America there has been a constant development for more than twenty years to make them (sports clothes) more beautiful. There has also been a trend to make sports clothing suitable for . . . all sorts of daytime functions or occasions.'[29] Nystrom claimed that 'American sports clothes style has set the fashion for the world. Paris creators have been slow in following up this lead.' By the 1930s, this inclination had emerged most strongly in California as a new fashion influence, associated with the less formal lifestyle of the West Coast and the bright colours of a sunny climate. Well-known trade names in the casual wear which emerged in this period include 'White Stag,' and 'Cole of California', who advertised in US *Vogue*. California became particularly famous for bathing suits and sports clothing, which even the French sometimes agreed was done better by the Americans; in 1940, the Paris-based designer Schiaparelli, then living in the US said 'It is amazing what America does with reasonably-priced clothes, especially sports clothes.'[30] A July 1932 US *Vogue* editorial, for example, illustrated a range of easy-to-wear garments made and sold in American department stores (figure 57). They include a 'knitted square, a fast trick for the beach', a bathing suit, a 'practical flannel suit', and 'wide and roomy flannel slacks'.

At the same time, the movies emerged in America, and surrounded by constant publicity, became an important vehicle for fashion dissemination to the masses.[31] Although Paris was an important influence on Hollywood design, and some French couturiers were employed to design costumes, the film industry also produced its own designers (such as Adrian), and the film costumes they created had a discernible independent accent. In the 1930s, a new generation of stars such as Katherine Hepburn starred in realistic comedies and introduced new down-to-earth, sporty ideals. This was a very different image from contemporary slinky Paris fashions. Nonetheless, it should be noted that other stars such as Jean Harlow represented alternative images of sultry sexuality, which can be seen as exaggerated and more dazzling versions of French style. Thus Hollywood films therefore displayed a range of clothing, mostly American-styled, which many people in America and Europe used as a personal guide.

In *New York Fashion: the Evolution of American Style*, Caroline Rennolds Milbank stresses the significance of 'practicality', 'comfort' and 'simplicity', as well as 'novelty' in US fashion, saying 'simplicity is an element of US fashion that cannot be overemphasised'.[32] Although recognition of the American style was slow to develop in the face of continued Paris deference, it accelerated noticeably during the Second World War. With France under enemy occupation, and no fashion reports for four years, American fashion magazines had no choice but to promote home style. Native designers such as Claire McCardell, who had been well known in the industry for years, came to public notice. In the inter-war years, McCardell had copied Paris fashions, but in the late 1930s and 1940s she became famous for producing understated and extremely inventive, easy-to-wear and well-made clothes at ready-to-wear level, with the attitude that 'clothes ought to be useful and comfortable'.[33] One of her best-known designs is a multi-coloured gingham playsuit, which was featured in *Harper's Bazaar* in 1942, and which bears a strong resemblance to the Italian playsuit by Mirsa seen in figure 38, yet predates it by fourteen years. Such casual clothes or 'sportswear' became more and more firmly associated with the 'American look'.[34] Soon after

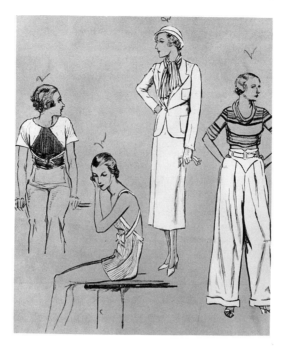

Figure 57. US Vogue editorial which illustrates a range of easy-to-wear garments made and sold in American department stores, including a 'knitted square, a fast trick for the beach', a bathing suit, a 'practical flannel suit', and 'wide and roomy flannel slacks'. Source: US Vogue, 1.7.32, pp. 56–7. Courtesy of Condé Nast Publications Inc.

wartime hostilities had ceased, *Life* wrote that 'The [American] ideal ... is the long-legged tennis-playing, swimming girl', under a title which claimed American innovation: 'Women Designers Set New Fashions'.

Immediately after the War, the relationships between American films and European audiences, and between European couture and the American market resumed. As in other European countries, many Italian magazines, such as *Grazia*, included editorials on Hollywood, its stars, and its costumes. Numerous screen garments were proposed for imitation, even if, at first, many of them were out of date, because of the post-war distribution of films made during the years of fascist autarky. In July 1946, for example, *Grazia* offered a pattern for a dress worn by Gene Tierney in Hitchcock's *Vertigo* of 1944. This represented a more practical and affordable version of Tierney's screen glamour, and illustrates an important method of transferral for American style to the Italian wardrobe.

The relationship between North American department stores and European couturiers is the context of a recent doctoral thesis by Alexandra Palmer.[35] Palmer states that once again, in this period, 'the North American fashion industry was dependent commercially and culturally on European couture designs; and the European couturiers were economically dependent on the North American market'. The new Italian couturiers and boutique designers were very much a part of this process, as this study shows. Although the immediate post-war years were actually a period of increasing liberation and casualness, fashion seemed to return to dressing up, rather than dressing down, at least for the first fifteen post-war years. With Dior's New Look, French couture returned to opulence, in contrast to the more 'sporty', simple feel of the dress of the 1920s, which had been such a strong look in America. Despite the eager American market for European style, and the keen acceptance of the New Look in the US, the American affinity with casuals was, if anything, more evident after the War. Commentators noticed that suburban living resulted in fresh versions of sportswear, designed for less active sports like tennis and golf, as well as what were termed 'playclothes': sundresses, shorts and long slim trousers.[36] As the Florentine paper *La Nazione* reported in July 1950, 'the taste of the US' was 'for simple things'.

Post-war US fashion style is summed up succinctly by the US magazine *Time*, which in May 1955 published an article entitled 'The American Look'. It was explained that 'in the US the meaning of elegance has changed as much as the meaning of leisure'. The dissimilarity between US lifestyle and French fashion style was addressed decisively: 'From America's lively leisure has evolved a new, home-grown fashion, as different from Paris fashion as apple pie from crepe suzette. Paris can still claim its true title as the custom-fashion capital of the world. But the French still design for Veblenesque leisure. Their clothes compliment the designer, whereas America's are made to compliment the wearer.' The report also pointed out that 'the demand for casual clothes has also become a mainstay of the vast and complex fashion business'.

An example of the American garments used to illustrate this point is seen in figure 58, a Clare Potter swimsuit 'in Persian Paisley print'. The writer went on to pinpoint the significance of McCardell, saying 'Claire McCardell started the casual American Look – comfort, function, simplicity and clean lines.' A selection of designs from McCardell's summer 1955 collection is shown in figure 59. The garments range from evening wear to bathing suits, and were described by *Time* as having 'the casual, functional American look.' Particularly important for this study, is that as early as 1955, it was noted that 'the American Look has had its influence abroad, particularly in Italy, where it has profoundly influenced the designers of sportswear'.

Significantly, a specific example of a direct relationship between American

Figure 58. Clare Potter swimsuit 'in Persian Paisley print' with matching wrap.
Source: *Time*, 2.5.55, p. 43.

'sportswear' and the evolving style of Italian fashion is found in US *Vogue* even earlier, in May 1951.[37] Under the title, 'Donna Simonetta Colonna and her $56 American Play Wardrobe', *Vogue* explained that the Italian designer Simonetta Visconti, of Rome (who was to become particularly well known for her sportswear), had 'bought her Summer-in-Capri wardrobe . . . in America . . . for 56 dollars'. *Vogue* also drew its readers' attention to an 'interesting point: that a woman with two continents to choose from, who is a designer herself, was so pleased with American play fashions and prices that she bought in this country her own wardrobe for a holiday summer in Italy.'

From the mid-1950s, youth fashions emerged. The US was one of the principal sources of the mainstream 'casual' trend which gave young people a very different look from that of their parents. Pleated skirts, bobby socks and twinsets presented a much more relaxed look than the stiff and mature formality of Paris-inspired suits. By the early 1960s, American magazines were shifting their emphasis from refined and mature fashions, to youthfulness and experimentation. US *Vogue* covered the new boutique scene and also

Figure 59. Garments from McCardell's Summer 1955 collection. Source: *Time,* 2.5.55, p. 39.

acted as a type of boutique itself, by using experimental stylists and designers, and by promoting the casual trend. This, according to the New York fashion PR, Eleanor Lambert, was America's 'lifestyle fashion'.[38] The compatibility of this trend with Italian style is summed up in a July 1960 *WWD* report, which described the production of a range of Simonetta's sportswear designs by New York ready-to-wear firm Arkin: 'the models were brought to the US by Mrs Cushman, the fashion editor of the Ladies Home Journal to be photographed for a two page promotion. Mrs Cushman selected the designs because she felt that they exemplified the way women want to dress.'

The two key themes in the American attitude to dress are 'simplicity' and 'glamour', and the similarity between these and Italian attitudes is also evident. Yet the stylistic relationship between the two countries was clearly more complex than a one-way, US to Italy impact. Despite having an immensely successful industrialised fashion sector and talented native designers, who were skilled at creating designs specifically in tune with the American lifestyle, this study has shown that from the early 1950s, Americans were keen to buy Italian garments in significant numbers.

Italy was offering something that was not available in America. Aside from the relative cheapness of Italian garments, it seems that this something was an essence of Italy, a cultural cachet, which was associated in the American mind with the history, tradition and style of Italy. America had traditionally bought its European style in great quantity from France. Paris style meant instant chic and stylistic leadership to the Americans, but in a specific, formal way, especially in the period of the New Look. In its colours and its simplicity, post-war Italian style fitted more easily into younger American lifestyles, whilst its often glittering evening elegance satisfied the American fondness for glamour. It could be said that the Italians took American casual sports-wear, injected it with freshness and sophistication and sold it back to America with the prestige of a European label.

US Encouragement to Italian Production to Style for US Requirements

There is no doubt that even in the late 1940s, at least some Italian designers were familiar with American preferences, and that some Italian fashion style was directed at the American market. The earliest firm indications of this are seen in the designs created for individual US film stars, from 1946, and in Pucci's sportswear, from 1947. Roman couturiers were mindful of the glamorous look traditionally favoured by Hollywood, and their gowns, especially the sumptuous evening gowns, reflected this. Moreover, Carla Strini explains that 'Pucci knew there were ladies in America who lived a different life, who led active lives, and wanted easier clothes; he knew that there was a market there. This knowledge came from the time he spent studying at Reed College in Oregon, just before the War, and from his international social circle.' Pucci's chic, easy-care, easy-wear designs were perfectly matched to this definition of the sartorial needs of many wealthy American women.

The earliest systematic targeting of the American market came with the launch of the Giorgini shows in 1951 for American buyers, as has been seen. Gianni Ghini (organiser of the presentations from 1952) recalls Giorgini's intentions for the American market very clearly, and states that 'there is no doubt that American taste had a strong influence'. As a long-standing exporter of Italian products to the American market, Giorgini was familiar with the American lifestyle and insisted that the designers separate themselves from French style in order to attract US sales. Although there is no evidence that his control over the particular direction of Italian style went further than this, his role was clearly pivotal. Once introduced to the US trade market by Giorgini, individual Italian designers were in a position to understand and respond to it.

As this study has shown, coverage of the trade between Italian designers and the US fashion industry in *WWD* provides a valuable insight into this relationship. At couture level it is clear that the selections made by US buyers had an important ad hoc impact on the styling of Italian fashion. It would have made poor business sense not to react to US preferences, when, as Settembrini points out, 'America represented between 70–80 per cent of the market for Italian fashionable clothing in the early years'.[39] Moreover, the creation of exclusive couture level collections for individual US stores, as reported in *WWD*, offers explicit evidence of formally contracted styling for US tastes.

It is at boutique level that the tailoring of Italian fashion style to the US market can be seen most clearly. It is no coincidence that Italian output of high quality sportswear increased, as the American fashion industry expounded its virtues. Moreover, several reports of particular instances can be found in *WWD* from the mid-1950s, beginning with knitwear. In October 1955, for example, the paper described 'a group of American-inspired two-piece ensembles at Curiel, recently returned from her trip to New York. These best-sellers include wool-jersey sheaths with matching cardigans.' A few months later, (February 1956) under the headline 'Italian knitwear producers expect exports to hit new high', the readership was told that 'Silk made for the American market differs in styling, colour and quality from those generally requested by Italian and European boutiques. American stores center on simple knitwear which has a casual look.' The continued targeting of the American market through adaptation to American style is summed up by a further report five years later, in October 1960 which explained that 'women in America are wearing sensible clothes', and this, it was claimed, was 'what the immediate future cycle will be – an increasing trend to the casual look'.

Italian sportswear designers not only tailored designs to US preferences, but created collections specially for the US in both formal and informal styles, as *WWD* announced in November 1956: 'To introduce Portofino clothes to the American market too, young designer Gianni Baldini has prepared a ready-to-wear collection of printed cotton skirts, slacks, pants, dresses and beachcoats, reported successful with commissionaires and resident buyers of leading US stores.' A few weeks after this, in December 1956, it was revealed that: 'Emilio, Mirsa, Glans, and Avagolf have designed for American buyers, special ranges of formal and daytime suits and coats, as well as outstanding separates for resort or sport and knitwear in wool and cotton.' These examples raise the issue of the extent of American encouragement to tailor Italian designs to US preferences.

A particularly interesting example of this intricate two-way stylistic relation-ship between America and Italy, was described at the boutique level fashion house Likis, by *WWD* in August 1956: 'Likis is a Milan house born after the War and dedicated to young socialites who like fresh-looking American-inspired ready-to-wear. The response is so good that the partners of the firm were convinced by New York manufacturer Anthony Blotta and by Enrico Costa, President of Tessitura Costa [an Italian textile house], to reverse their formula and prepare seasonal collections of ready-to-wear with Italian flavour for the US market'. This report shows that in at least one case, Italian fashion had deliberately assimilated American style and sold it to the Italian market, and then in turn had been encouraged by an Italian textile manufacturer and an American fashion house to sell the Italian version of that style to the US. The continued input of the American fashion trade in the design of many Italian ranges is revealed by *WWD*'s December 1961 comment that 'Italian manufacturers note that many American buyers accompany Italian ready-to-wear manufacturers to choose fabrics for sportswear and ready-to-wear to be made in Italy for the US market.'

Florentine buyer Enzo Tayar was a middle man in many such negotiations in the 1945–65 period, and testifies that in his experience at the boutique and quality ready-to-wear level, the American input went much further than the selection of fabrics: 'the designs were strictly styled for the Americans; the buyers conveyed the requirements, came up with colours, and so on'.[40] In 1952/3, for example, Tayar remembers cut and sewn poplin shirts for women being made for the American market, and states that 'the styling came from the US, and followed from the success of Pucci in the American market'. The compliance of Italian manufacturers, he says, was 'the key to Italian success', because 'they accepted the US way of doing business, and went out of their way to adapt, because if they didn't, they didn't get the business'.

Tayar defines this intricate process as 'like a dog biting its own tail. The American buyers came to Italy for ideas, but then adapted those ideas for their own markets, and then gave them back to the Italian vendors to make in their colours, size specs etc.' The awareness of the Italian fashion industry of such requirements can be seen in figure 60, a *Linea Maglia* editorial from autumn 1954, entitled 'The fashion and holidays that foreigners prefer', which shows a range of boutique knitwear designed by Mirsa, against a backdrop of posters designed for the Italian Tourist Office which encourage foreigners to, for example, spend the 'Summer in Italy'.

Even at Italian manufacturers, such as MaxMara, which did not sell in the American market, design could be modified in accordance with US stylistic developments. By the mid-1960s, MaxMara's major manufacturing problems had been ironed out and the emerging issue was one of image. At the same time, Evan Picone, an Italian-American 7th Avenue contact from the early 1950s, produced an ensemble of checked jacket, flannel skirt, and red knit top, which MaxMara's founder Achille Maramotti noticed in their catalogue, together with fabric swatches, and options.[41] This was the first 'Total Look'

La moda e le vacanze
che gli stranieri preferiscono

Quattro esemplari di maglieria
a mano
creati dalla Mirsa.

Pullover con bordi fantasia
laterali
e berretto intonato.

Maglione sportivo
con maniche a raglan sottolineata
da profili vivaci.

Giacchino bicolore a punto rado
e giacchino rosso a larghe
coste.

Figure 60. Knitted tops by Mirsa, featured in an article entitled 'The Fashion and the Holidays the Foreigners Prefer'. Source: *Linea Maglia*, Autumn 1954, p. 38.

that Maramotti had witnessed. MaxMara still only had the ability to produce coats and suits, but through these developments in American ready-to-wear, he saw the need for a co-ordinated image, which has since become the symbol of Italian fashion.

MaxMara established separate factories for making dresses and other additional garments and by the end of 1967, had evolved the concept of the 'Total Look' collection, with the new label 'Sportmax'. The idea was that the customer could buy just a few complementary garments, which she could put together in different ways to create different outfits for any occasion. This was directed at a new market of young women aged 18 to 30. Maramotti was the first in Italy, he says, to realise that image was vital, and that fashion manufacturers could no longer sell just 'a skirt' or 'a coat'. He saw that he needed to propose an identifiable personality: 'the romantic woman', 'the sporty woman' or 'the aggressive woman', within the broader MaxMara message, which remained 'stylish, simple, subtle and smart'. Although MaxMara style began as a translation of the Paris look, it became independent of French haute couture in the mid-1960s and by 1965 can be said to fit neatly into the 'low-key elegance' category for which Italian high fashion was increasingly known.

Stylistic change in the Italian clothing industry, at couture, boutique, and quality ready-to-wear level, was predominantly led by the requirements of the American market. It is evident that the American fashion industry played a major and stimulating role in this process. Even before the export of Italian fashion to America took off in the 1950s, Italian designers were known to tailor garments to the preferences of their American clientele. From this period, and increasingly, in the 1950s, American department stores commissioned exclusive collections from Italian couturiers and boutique designers. By the mid-1950s, American manufacturers were beginning to control styling, which was accepted by Italian producers, in return for the scale of the business. Furthermore, such was the complexity of the links between the American and Italian fashion industries, that ready-to-wear manufacturer MaxMara assimilated important changes in stylistic direction from America, although this was not instigated by the American source.

The Promotion of Italian Fashion to America

As we have seen, the reputation of Italian fashion was firmly rooted in high quality and traditional associations; casual sportswear became casual elegance. This reputation was the key to the promotion of Italian fashion in the US in the 1945–65 period. There is no evidence that Italian fashion designers or manufacturers paid for advertising in the US in these years. However, using predominantly a mixture of social events, aristocratic associations and designer visits, Italian fashion sold the idea of Italy's culture and heritage to America. This issue has been addressed by a number of writers, most notably by Valerie Steele in *Italian Metamorphosis 1943–68*.[42] The readings offered by such writers can be confirmed by the oral testimonies of Micol Fontana, Gianni Ghini and Carla Strini, as well as reports in the US press.

Although Italian fashion style centred on a pared-down modern look, tradition was the vital context for its promotion. Even the first important Italian fashion show of the post-war period, at the Teatro della Pergola in Florence in May 1950, utilised Italy's tradition of art and culture, as models emerged from reproductions of famous Renaissance paintings. Giorgini's

Florentine shows were also redolent with historical connotations. Florence itself was one of Italy's most famous centres of culture, and the shows were presented initially at Giorgini's own ancient palazzo, and from 1952, in the Sala Bianca at the imposing Pitti Palace. The Palazzo Strozzi, another famous Florentine monument, was used as a couturier showroom during the presentations. Gianni Ghini, who was instrumental in the organisation of the shows, recalls that it was Giorgini's intention to make the presentations as grand and formal as possible, with all men in black tie. This grandeur was aimed specifically at the US audience, as British fashion journalist Ernestine Carter wrote in her autobiography: 'In Florence, the American journalists got the V.I.P. treatment. For them cars and drivers were provided . . . while the rest of us sloshed off in the rain.'[43] Carter's recollections, with regard to Giorgini's attitude to American buyers and press, are corroborated by Bianca Maria Piccinino, an Italian television journalist, who attended the Florentine presentations: 'He was a gentleman and knew how to treat people incredibly well. He would greet and welcome his guests from all over the world, but especially the Americans, who were so very important then. He would make them feel like foreign princes.'[44]

Giorgini also staged an impressive support system of social events at the time of the shows, such as grand historic balls set in magnificent locations, for the entertainment of foreign press and buyers, which were intended to link fashion to Italy's cultural significance. Gianni Ghini states that although 'not one cent was paid for promotion, press or publicity, the Giorgini historical balls were much talked about in the press and ultimately offered excellent publicity'. Moreover, the balls meant immediate sales for the couturiers, as Giorgini explained in July 1952: 'the goal of the evening is to show our fashion to advantage; the ladies are requested to wear garments of pure Italian inspiration'. One example worn at the previous season's ball was reported in *WWD*, in January 1952, when 'Mrs Hannah Troy wore this striking black and white gown from Veneziani at the Giorgini ball.' The worth of such early publicity in the American fashion trade press was inestimable.

Surviving film footage, entitled 'July 1952, La Settimana Incom: Moda a Palazzo Pitti', itself intended as publicity, provides an excellent example of Giorgini's approach to such promotion.[45] This film of the July 1952 presentations begins with panoramic views of Florence seen from the famous Belvedere, followed by a horse and carriage crossing the famous Piazza Santa Croce, and an evocative voice-over which explains: 'In the morning light in Florence, the carriages clatter past the Lungarno and over the Ponte Vecchio to the Pitti Palace. But the arrival of the visitors is somehow different. The salute of the guards sent by the city government indicates that these are guests of honour.' The narrator links this celebration of foreign buyers and press to

Italy's cultural heritage by saying 'it is easy to understand how the arts have blossomed in Florence, it reaches out to make the arts grow. Fashion may be an applied art, but like any other art it flourishes where the climate is favourable.' This accompanied shots of American journalists being carried up steep cobbled streets in sedan chairs to a medieval banquet.

Maria Pezzi, illustrator and journalist, recalls the editor of US *Vogue*, Bettina Ballard, saying of Italian fashion that 'we may not agree on all the materials, but we are in a wonderful city, with courteous people who invite us into their homes and offer us things that we cannot find elsewhere'. A devotee of Paris fashion, Ballard wrote of the early Italian shows in her autobiography: 'I could feel the waves of pros and cons rising and falling in the soft Florentine air, the pros winning because it was so manifestly attractive to discover fashion in a country so full of treasures to see and eat, and people who were so polite and open-armed'.[46] Giorgini's tactics were evidently effective.

Allied to the importance of grandeur and culture in the presentation of Italian fashion to the US fashion trade and press were its strong aristocratic associations. Not only were the foreigners serenaded in historic locations and with courtly entertainments, they were often sold fashions by noble personages. Many of the Italian designers were themselves of aristocratic birth, including Simonetta, Galitzine, and Pucci, and this imbued these individual houses, and indeed, the whole of Italian fashion, with valuable kudos in the US, a relatively new country, which had no such ancient class distinction. Even before the end of wartime hostilities, Bettina Ballard sent her photographs of Italian aristocrats, such as the Princess Galitzine, back to US *Vogue*, which published them and 'started the rage for barefoot sandals in America'.[47] Those involved in Italian fashion were well aware of the significance of aristocratic kudos, and Sorelle Fontana, for example, who had no blue blood, engaged Galitzine in the late 1940s, who spoke several languages, to liaise with the American market.

The 'free' promotion of Italian fashion to the international, and especially American, market, did not end on Italian soil. Both individual designers, and official groups visited the US regularly. The publicity value of such trips was two-fold, with both official press coverage of the planned promotional events, and the added bonus of eager press coverage of related social events. Micol Fontana and Emilio Pucci are excellent examples of a couture and a boutique designer who maximised such interest. Micol Fontana was responsible for the American trade at Sorelle Fontana, and was tireless in her quest for publicity there. Although Fontana's earliest links with the US market were through Hollywood, and her earliest visit to the US in 1951, was as a guest of Hollywood stars, from this starting point, she made many trips aimed at the US fashion trade market. By 1995, she had been to America ninety-four times, and is clear that *WWD* coverage was the key to the American press: 'Once you have been in *WWD*, they all want an interview. After that, I was in all the papers, and I went on American television a lot.' The regularity of her visits, and consequent publicity is revealed in a *WWD* report of 1956, which announced that 'Micol Fontana is on her way to the US again. This time to receive an award from the Pittsburgh Fashion Group. Ten gowns of the Fontana spring collection will be modelled by Pittsburgh society women.' A few months later, *WWD* described another Fontana visit: 'Micol Fontana has left for New York to present her export collection there at the end of April.'

However, Fontana states that once the initial interest was generated by early *WWD* coverage of the Fontana collections, promotion in the US came 'mainly socially and through business meetings'. Fontana remembers 'big parties at the Italian embassy and being received at the White House by Eisenhower'. By this time, Fontana were dressing not only film stars, but also important clients from the world of politics. The importance of such social events is underlined by the seasoned fashion PR Eleanor Lambert, who states that 'Italian fashion names [usually of great social standing] were an important part of American high life. They were at the parties, looking wonderful, they got a lot of press attention, and people at the parties wanted to look like them.'

Carla Strini, Emilio Pucci's 'Head of Foreign Operations', recollects a similar pattern at Pucci, saying that 'Pucci was an exceptional PR for himself', and knew that his main market was in the US.[48] Strini was employed by Pucci specifically to deal with such foreign trade, and 'to free him to go to America as often as was necessary'. Pucci 'already had a lot of social contacts because of his noble position', and went to the US predominantly to cultivate these and to develop business with the US fashion trade, especially the large department stores. Strini states that 'Pucci went to the States at least once a month after I joined, despite the fact that the trip took at least ten hours, stopping at Rekjavik and Ireland.' She explains that 'he would take his models with him, and the clothes were shipped ahead. Pucci organised the shows, usually at department stores, and decided how to present the clothes.' Clearly, Pucci's personality played a central role in the promotion of his garments to America. Strini also relates Pucci's attendance at glittering parties ' full of VIP's', with all his models dressed in his designs, which offered excellent publicity; if America's most important and most wealthy society women knew about, talked about and wore Pucci, then the lower social echelons would want to emulate them. Furthermore, the high-profile and elegant editors of the American fashion press also wore Pucci's clothes to similar effect. Strini is unsure whether Pucci actually gave his garments to such women, but she does remember that he sent them accessories, such as scarves, in the Pucci trademark vivid prints.

Although Pucci and Fontana were tireless self-publicists and can be seen as pioneers of the promotion of Italian fashion in America, their experiences are not atypical. According to Bettina Ballard, for example, Simonetta was 'the best business person in the Italian couture'.[49] Ballard wrote in 1960 that Simonetta 'has toured America, doing gruelling one-night stands promoting her perfume and her clothes'. In October 1961, *WWD* revealed that Fabiani was in New York on his 'fifteenth visit', to promote his collection, albeit in a somewhat more light-hearted vein: 'he's here to have fun, see people, and to watch the girls on 5th Avenue'. Nor were such visits the reserve of the top-level couture and boutique, at least by the mid-1960s. In October 1963, representatives of Milanese quality ready-to-wear manufacturer Likis were in New York to promote its spring collection, and were recorded by *WWD*: 'it is their second trip to the US and it marks the interest of American stores for medium priced garments with an Italian flavour'.

Publicity was not left to the individual efforts of designers alone. In February 1955, *WWD* reported that 'Italy group flies to US tomorrow for style telecast'. The paper explained the formal nature of the visit: 'Giorgini, with four Italian mannequins, flies to New York tomorrow via Pan-Am. He will stay at the Savoy Plaza as a guest of the National Broadcasting Company. Mr Giorgini will present a televised collection of 24 models from Antonelli, Capucci, Carosa, Schuberth, and Fabiani, all of Rome, and Marucelli and Veneziani of Milan, as well as a smaller collection from boutique houses.' It is highly significant that the Italian models for the presentation were 'six Contessas and two Marchesas', as it was reported by *Look* magazine. Italian fashion was presented as the height of aristocratic elegance to the vast American television audience.

As well as collective promotional visits organised by Giorgini, other promotional events were arranged by official bodies such as the Italian embassy, often in conjunction with US department stores. These events were duly reported in the American press. In October 1960, for example, *WWD* described 'Italian fashions in great variety worn by guests attending the Italian Ambassador's Ball, which officially opened the Neiman-Marcus Italian Fortnight in Dallas'. The report included mention of a Fontana gown worn by Mrs Peter Travis of New York. Department stores played a central role in the promotion of Italian fashion, because they were the major retailers, and understood the value of publicity.

The stores organised many promotions such as the Neiman-Marcus Italian Fortnight, and encouraged the designers' presence at the event. In March

1955, for example, *WWD* told how Veneziani had visited New York 'at the invitation of a leading New York retailer', and took 'a collection of winter models exclusively designed for this store'.

Five years later, the Neiman-Marcus Fortnight involved a score of Italian couture and sportswear designers who showed half a dozen styles each. Gresy, Pucci and Camerino personally participated in the festival, showing collections designed especially for the event. This occasion was not unusual. In the same year, *WWD* listed six stores, from across the US, which were due to stage Italian promotions in the autumn, including Jordan Marsh of Boston, Stern Brothers of New York, and Bon Marché in Seattle. Another report the following year indicates that such promotions were the result of co-operation between stores and designers, in mutual interest, and were not solely instigated by the stores. Laura Aponte, for example, toured the US in February 1961 with her entire spring collection. Aponte had arranged visits to New York, Detroit, Chicago, San Francisco, and Dallas, but by 23 January only had promotions assured at Saks 5th Avenue and Neiman Marcus.

The representation of Italian fashion in the non-trade US fashion press is also important here and has been addressed recently by Valerie Steele, in *Italian Metamorphosis 1943–68* (1994). Steele describes the way in which designs were often promoted in conjunction with stories about holidays in Italy, in a stereotypically touristic way. Typical titles published by US *Vogue* include 'Italian Ideas for any South' (November 1951), and in March 1954, 'Renaissance in Italian Design', which was accompanied by 'Four Young Italian Beauties', and a 'Travel Tip sheet'. One of the earliest articles on Italian fashion in US *Vogue* was 'The Fine Italian Hand', of September 1946. The illustrations were shot in Rome, in palaces and at ancient sites, and the fashions by designers such as Galitzine, Gattinoni and Fontana, were worn by aristocratic socialites, including Countess Sandra Spaletti and Countess 'Niki' Visconti. The models appeared like ancient statuary in the niches of classical architecture, and the text was loaded with stereotypical generalisations of the Italian people and culture. Examples of this include 'Italian women are endowed with beautiful legs and feet, possibly the best in Europe', 'the Italian woman of breeding also has a certain quality of relaxation [not unnatural, since she seldom works], which endows her clothes with an easy grace,' and 'the gilded palaces of Rome . . . demand clothes in the grand manner'. The American idea of Italy's grand and noble heritage, and the importance of aristocratic connections are clearly evident here.

Even more specific was *Life* magazine's first coverage of Italian fashion in a report entitled 'Italy Gets Dressed Up', just a few weeks after the second Italian fashion show organised by Giorgini, in 1951. Again models were photographed at Rome's ancient sites, in both evening wear and daywear as in figure 3, a Fabiani coat shot in the colonnades at St Peter's. Simonetta was described as 'the titled glamour girl of Italian designers', with 'clothes designed especially for lounging Americans'. The article was illustrated with a photograph of the designers, shown in a group on a Florence street, including 'six assorted titles' and another of the young Italian socialite Arabella LeMaitre 'shown wearing a sports outfit of narrow slacks, poplin raincoat and patent hat from Veneziani, with omnipresent open sandals'.

Conclusion

Whilst Italians involved in Italian fashion certainly promoted their product to the American market using the tools of social events, aristocratic associations, culture, heritage, and designer visits, it cannot be denied that Americans involved in selling Italian fashion to the American consumer were equally happy to appropriate and enhance them. Specifically, the American press was instrumental in conveying this idea of Italy and Italian fashion to the American consumer.

Notes

1. Gramsci, Antonio, *Sections from the Prison Notebooks*, Lawrence and Wishart, London, 1971.

2. This chronology is addressed by Forgacs, David, *Culture in the Industrial Era 1880–1980: Cultural Industries, Politics and the Public*, Manchester University Press, Manchester, 1990, p. 2.

3. See Sparke, Penny, 'Industrial Design or Industrial Aesthetics?: American Influence on the Emergence of the Italian Modern Design Movement, 1948–58', in Duggan, Christopher and Wagstaff, Christopher (eds), *Italy in the Cold War: Politics, Culture and Society, 1948–58*, Berg, Oxford, 1995, pp. 159–67. For further details of the development of Italian design, see Sparke, Penny, *Italian Design 1870 to the Present Day*, Thames and Hudson, London, 1988.

4. For an account of American industrial design, see Meikle, Jeffrey L., *Twentieth Century Limited: Industrial Design in America, 1925–39*, Temple, Philadelphia, 1979.

5. Sparke, Penny, 'Industrial Design or Industrial Aesthetics?: American Influence on the Emergence of the Italian Modern Design Movement, 1948–58', in Duggan, Christopher and Wagstaff, Christopher (eds), *Italy in the Cold War: Politics, Culture and Society, 1948–58*, Berg, Oxford, 1995, p. 161.

6. For further details, see the Italian design magazine *Domus*, which Ponti founded in 1928, until the War, and edited once more from 1947 and Liatra Ponti, Lisa, *Gio Ponti: the Complete Work 1923–1978*, Thames and Hudson, London, 1990.

7. See for example, Radice, Barbara, *Ettore Sottsass: a Critical Biography*, Thames and Hudson, London, 1993, and Sparke, Penny, *Ettore Sottsass Jnr.*, Design Council, London, 1982.

8. Sparke, Penny, 'Industrial Design or Industrial Aesthetics?: American Influence on the Emergence of the Italian Modern Design Movement, 1948–58', in Duggan, Christopher and Wagstaff, Christopher (eds), *Italy in the Cold War: Politics, Culture and Society, 1948–58*, Berg, Oxford, 1995, p. 165.

9. The notions of the 'nation' and 'national culture' were very important in the elite discourse of the period. The most typical contemporary approach to cultural change in the post-war years was to view the advent of 'Americanised' mass culture in Italy in negative terms. See for example, Fortini, Franco, 'Il Senno di Poi', in *Deici Inverni 1947–57: Contributi ad un Discorso Socialista*, De Donato, Bari, 1973, p. 33. Fortini stated in 1957 that 'the crudest forms of the American way of life, initially disseminated by the mass culture industry, will soon change into more subtle and dangerous reformist enterprises'. For a range of contemporary assessments, see for example, Baranski, Z.G. and Lumley, R., (eds), *Culture and Conflict in Post-War Italy: Essays on Mass and Popular Culture*, Macmillan, London, 1990, and Ellwood, David. W., *Rebuilding Western Europe: America and Post-War Reconstruction*, Longman, London, 1992.

10. Massai interview, Milan, 19.7.95.

11. Hughes, H.S., *The United States and Italy*, Harvard University Press, Cambridge, Mass./London, 1979, p. 12.

12. Ellwood, David. W., *Rebuilding Western Europe: America and Post-War Reconstruction*, Longman, London, 1992, p. 227.

13. Gundle, Stephen, 'The Americanisation of Daily Life: Television and Consumerism in Italy in the 1950s', in *Italian Culture and Society*, 2, 1996, pp. 11–38. This is a revised version of an article that first appeared in Italian in *Quaderni Storici*, 62, XXI, 2, 1986, pp. 561–90. Although the roots of Italy's cultural transformation can be traced to the pre-Second World War years, Gundle identifies the post-war years as the key transitional period, due to 'Italy's low level of economic development in the early 1950s, and the rapidity of change in immediately successive years'.

14. *Culture in the Industrial Era 1880–1980: Cultural Industries, Politics and the Public*, Manchester University Press, 1990, p. 1. Forgacs defines modernisation in this context as designating 'the passage from a traditional society to one characterised by industrial capitalism, and by the social and political forms associated with it'.

15. Schiller, Herbert, *Mass Communications and American Empire*, New York, 1960, quoted in Gundle, Stephen, 'The Americanisation of Daily Life: Television and Consumerism in Italy in the 1950s', in *Italian Culture and Society*, 2, 1996, p. 39.

16. Brunetta, Gian Piero, 'The Long March of American Cinema in Italy from Fascism to the Cold War', in *Hollywood in Europe: Experiences of a Cultural Hegemony*, (eds) Ellwood, David, and Kroes, Rob, VU University Press, Amsterdam, 1994.

17. Presented at a conference entitled 'The Politics of Power: Italy in the Cold War Period', at Reading University, 26–7 October 1990, and published in Duggan, Christopher and Wagstaff, Christopher (eds), *Italy in the Cold War: Politics, Culture and Society 1948–58*, Berg, Oxford, 1995, pp. 89–109.

18. *Italy in the Cold War: Politics, Culture and Society 1948–58*, ibid., p. 95. This compares to UK figures of 1635 million in 1946, which fell to 1182 million in 1955.

19. Ellwood, David and Kroes, Rob, *Hollywood in Europe: Experiences of a Cultural Hegemony*, VU University Press, Amsterdam, 1994, p. 153.

20. Gundle, Stephen, 'The Americanisation of Daily Life: Television and Consumerism in Italy in the 1950s', in *Italian Culture and Society*, 2, 1996, p. 38.

21. Bianchino, Gloria, 'From Drawing to Design', in Butazzi, Grazietta et al, *Italian Fashion, Volume 1: The Origins of High Fashion and Knitwear*, Electa, Milan,1987, p. 116.

22. Fontana archive, customer records, include for example; n. 1/F Loy pure silk and printed tulle evening dress; n. 37/F Kelly silk organdie evening dress; n.2/F Taylor black and white silk crepe, piquet and velvet evening dress; n.21/F Gardner evening dress in ottoman silk.

23. Fontana Archive; n.4/F Kennedy.

24. Brooklyn Museum, 54205.

25. See also, for example, Franciolini's 'Il mondo le condanna' (1953), De Santis' 'Un marito per Anna Zaccheo' (1953), and Antonioni's 'Le amiche' (1953).

26. Fontana, Micol, *Specchio a Tre Luci*, Nuova Eri, Turin, 1991, p. 88.

27. Ibid., p88.

28. This is exemplified by the 'Gibson Girl', a cartoon created by American Charles Dana Gibson in the late nineteenth century, who played sport and usually wore a simple skirt and blouse combination.

29. Nystrom, Paul, *The Economics of Fashion*, Ronald Press, New York, 1928, p. 377.

30. Quoted in Kidwell, Claudia B. and Christman, Margaret C., *Suiting Everyone: the Democratisation of Clothing in America*, Smithsonian Institute, Washington D.C., 1974, p. 169.

31. For further details of the impact of Hollywood on women's dress, see De la Haye, Amy, 'Hollywood's Influence on the Development of Women's Ready-to-Wear Fashion in the USA, 1930–39', unpublished BA (Hons) thesis, University of Brighton, 1984.

32. Rennolds Milbank, Caroline, *New York Fashion: the Evolution of American Style*, Abrams, New York, 1989.

33. Claire McCardell, quoted in Lee Levin, Phyliss, *The Wheels of Fashion*, Doubleday, New York, 1965, p. 224. For further details see McCardell, Claire, *What Shall I Wear? The What, Where, When and How Much of Fashion*, New York, 1956; Steele, Valerie, *Women of Fashion: Twentieth Century Designers*, Rizzoli, New York, 1991, pp. 103–13, and Yohannan, Kohle, *Claire McCardell: Redefining Modernism*, Harry N. Abrams, New York, 1998.

34. Used in this context, the term sportswear does not describe clothes designed for sport, but conveys the casual feeling associated with the 'American look'. Examples of other American designers working in this field include Georgia Kay, Clare Potter, Tina Lesser, Tom Brigance and Carolyn Schurner.

35. Palmer, Alexandra, 'The Myth and Reality of Haute Couture: Consumption, Social Function and Taste in Toronto, 1945–1963', doctoral thesis, University of Brighton, 1994.

36. Rennolds Milbank, Caroline, *New York Fashion: the Evolution of American Style*, Abrams, New York, 1989 p. 179.

37. 'Donna Simonetta Colonna and her $56 American Play Wardrobe', US *Vogue*, 15.5.51, page unknown.

38. Eleanor Lambert, fashion PR, now in her nineties, in interview, New York, 24.8.94.

39. Settembrini interview, Florence, 17.10.95.

40. Tayar interview, Florence, 18.10.95.

41. Maramotti interview, Reggio Emilia, 21.7.95.

42. Steele, Valerie, 'Italian Fashion and America', in Celant, Germano, (ed.), *Italian Metamorphosis 1943–68*, Guggenheim, New York, 1994, pp. 497–502.

43. Carter, Ernestine, *With Tongue in Chic*, Michael Joseph, London, 1974, p. 128.

44. Piccinino, Bianca Maria, speaking on 'La Sala Bianca' (Video), VideoCast/Pitti Immagine, Florence, 1992.

45. Original film footage: 'July 1952, La Settimana Incom: Moda a Palazzo Pitti', presented as part of 'La Sala Bianca' (Video), VideoCast/Pitti Immagine, Florence, 1992.

46. Ballard, Bettina, *In My Fashion*, Secker and Warburg, London, 1960, p. 244.

47. Ibid., p. 184.

48. Strini interview, near Florence, 18.10.95.

49. Ballard, Bettina, *In My Fashion*, Secker and Warburg, London, 1960, p. 256.

Conclusion

The contribution of America to the early development of the Italian fashion industry, in terms of America's initial financial support and close involvement in the industrial organisation of Italy, as a supplier of progressive manufacturing methods, as a cultural model, and as a keen market, is much more profound than has previously been acknowledged. Further, the US played a specific role in the post-war success of the Italian textile industry, by ensuring regeneration through US markets and its Aid programmes (and to a lesser extent, and for a shorter time, through its technology). The Italian textile industry in turn was decisive in the development of the Italian fashion industry, in terms of promotion, flexibility and innovation. A systematic, mutually advantageous and economically significant relationship between the two industries developed rapidly from the early 1950s.

This study has demonstrated that quality women's ready-to-wear clothing was not only made in Italy very soon after the War, but that by the end of the 1950s this was being exported to the US in significant quantities. In the Italian post-war shift towards ready-to-wear production, Italy learnt many lessons from the American fashion industry, because American production was already automated on a large scale and was already geared towards rapid stylistic change. Moreover, as the most important market for Italian high fashion, American buyers, especially retailers, moulded Italian design and production to their requirements. An understanding of an Italian 'look' was a commercial reality for these buyers, and this has been clearly demonstrated in the descriptive language used in both the trade and popular press.

Until the end of the 1950s, when Italian ready-to-wear production expanded and developed, the US market was interested predominantly in high fashion Italian imports. Garments were not only bought for resale in the US. Italian designers were commissioned specifically to produce exclusive collections for US retailers, and many Italian designs were sold for reproduction by both retailers and manufacturers in America. As the 1950s progressed, Italian ready-made boutique garments, including knitwear, were purchased in increasing quantity for sale in the US. The possibilities of volume production were demonstrated to Italian high fashion designers through these US connections, whilst more and more Italian couturiers produced ready-to-wear collections and more and more high-quality ready-to-wear was exported.

From the early 1950s, a group of middle to high-quality ready-to-wear manufacturers were emerging in Italy, at the level below boutique. A number of these companies began their export drives in America, often at the very start of their ready-to-wear production. This is a highly significant group, because many of the companies which emerged in the early to mid-1950s, such as MaxMara, were to become central to the celebrated expansion and international success of Italian high quality ready-to-wear fashion from the late 1970s. US expertise and technology was crucial to the expansion of these manufacturers, through the use of US contacts, employment of American personnel, and the appropriation of production techniques from dealings with US retailers and manufacturers.

Little original fashion design has been identified in the pre-1945 period and certainly there was no internationally recognised unified 'Italian Look'. French couture continued to be seen as the epitome of style and the leader of international fashion. The first collective Italian presentations in 1951 mark a deliberate attempt to sever Italian stylistic dependency on Paris, and awaken the international market to Italian fashion design. Through examination of scores of examples of Italian garments, this study has shown that whilst Italian couture was not obviously different from Paris fashions in terms of cut, the now well-known Italian attitude to surface decoration, colour and fabric treatment was already evident in the early collections of the 1950s. Even more importantly, it was from this point that Italy's boutique fashions began to be presented to and noticed by an influential international audience. The casual style of Italian boutique clothing was seen as very different from the formality of the couture and especially from the more prescriptive grandeur of French couture. Boutique design was seen by international buyers as the most stylistically interesting sector of Italian fashion for its ease, colour, fabric and innovation, and it is this sector which most obviously pointed the way forward towards the mass-produced, fashionable, high-quality casuals for which Italy is so famous today.

Easy-to-wear, elegant casuals were ideally suited to meet the demands of social change in the 1945–65 period, as the lives of rich women relaxed, and the market for good quality fashion expanded. This look was particularly well received in America, where it was seen to equate to US attitudes to dress, and to meet a demand for high-style casuals. Italian fashion offered a younger, fresher, more colourful, and often more elegant alternative to US high-style casuals. Evidently the foundations for Italy's late twentieth century success in the sphere of 'casual elegance' were laid during the 1950s and early 1960s, and there was indeed an internationally recognisable and recognised

'Italian style' by the end of this period. Pucci's October 1960 prediction reported by *WWD*, 'Pucci Sees Couture Doom, Ties High Fashion to Ready-to-Wear' was an accurate one; at the end of the twentieth century, mainstream Italian fashion is known precisely for its understated elegance, and it is in this national stylistic identity that the secret of Italy's fashion success lies.

The significant relationship between US style and the emerging 'Italian Look' is also rooted in the broader cultural relationship between the two nations. American cultural attitudes, including the growth of popular mass-consumption, were a potent force amongst the Italian people and by the 1950s, it is clear that both manufacturers and consumers were generally eager to adopt American cultural models. As has been seen, since Italian fashion output was initially directed predominantly at the American market, Italian fashion design was often specifically moulded to American taste. The best publicised example of this was the creation of glamorous designs for Hollywood film stars at couture level, but the impact of US taste was felt within all the market levels analysed in this study.

It may be concluded that the requirements of the American market played a vital role in stimulating Italian stylistic change, especially through the responses of designers and manufacturers who sold to America. These were predominantly those at couture and boutique level. Highly significant instances have been identified showing American manufacturers controlling Italian styling by the mid-1950s.

However, although Italian fashion drew on American style in this way and especially on the notion of casual sportswear, the industry combined this with its own native Italian traditions. Assessment of the promotion of Italian fashion to America shows that the Italian fashion industry actively sold its designs in the context of Italy's cultural heritage, and that American retailers and manufacturers used similar tools in their own promotions of Italian fashion. Italian fashion was seen very much in the context of its traditional associations. By 1965 it was perceived internationally as of commercially viable high quality, and was already known for its stylish 'casual elegance'. This term both springs from and is distinct from the notion of American casual sportswear.

Finally, it is now evident that the history of Italian post-war fashion did not begin in the 1970s, and that in terms of financial support, the industrial organisation of Italy, manufacturing methods, cultural models, and markets, Italy took a crucial lead from America, and that long-term lessons were learnt in the 1945–65 period. America, however, did not entirely control the process, nor was Italy an unwilling pawn. The Italian fashion industry responded enthusiastically to US demand. The process was of mutual benefit, and between the original inspiration and the end result, there was much adaptation and interpretation. The results of this research thus add further weight to the argument that Americanisation in post-war Italy was a complicated process, in which domestic energies and inspirations made use of American ideas and technologies but on their own terms and without necessarily being dominated by them.

By 1965, the Italian fashion industry was growing in confidence and developing its own manufacturing techniques and style. By the early 1970s, Italy was successfully promoting a quality image for its ready-to-wear on the international market, through concentration on brands and designer, whilst improving production technology. By the mid-1970s the way was paved for the emergence of an internationally important, and stylistically independent fashion industry, led by precisely this élite ready-to-wear sector and by the early 1980s, Italy was being heralded by the international fashion press as one of the top three players on the international fashion stage. It is specifically the quality ready-to-wear section of the clothing market which has remained Italy's forte to the present day. This research has proved that the two decades following the Second World War were critical to the establishment of today's celebrated Italian fashion industry, and that the USA played a deeply significant and as yet unacknowledged role in this development. At the start of a new millenium, in an era in which nations are struggling to preserve and develop their cultural identities, it is important that the roots of the Italian fashion industry (an industry which is now such a powerful icon of Italian national identity) be properly recognised and understood.

Select Bibliography

Abruzzo, A. (1989), *Facis, Sidi, Cori: un' Analisi Condotta sui Fondi dell'Archivio Storico sulla Grafica e la Pubblicita dal 1954 al 1979*, Turin, GFT.

Asor-Rosa, A. (1975), 'La Cultura', *Storia d'Italia*, vol. 14, 'Dall' Unità a Oggi', 2, Turin, Einaudi.

Aynsley, J. (1993), *Nationalism and Internationalism: Design in the Twentieth Century*, London, V&A.

Ballard, B. (1960), *In my Fashion*, London, Secker and Warburg.

Baranski, Z.G. and Lumley, R. (eds) (1990), *Culture and Conflict in Post-War Italy: Essays on Mass and Popular Culture*, London, Macmillan.

Becker, J. and Knipping, F. (eds) (1986), *Power in Europe: Great Britain, France, Italy, and Germany in a Postwar World 1945–50*, Berlin and New York, De Gruyter.

Berta, G. (ed.) (1987), *Appunti sull'Evoluzione del Gruppo GFT: Un'Analisi Condotta sui Fondi dell'Archivio Storico*, Turin, GFT.

Bianchino, G. (ed.) (1984), *Sorelle Fontana*, Parma, CSAC.

Bianchino, G. (1987), *Italian Fashion Designing, 1945–1980*, Parma, CSAC.

Bradford De Long, J. and Eichengreen, B. (May 1992), *The Marshall Plan: History's Most Successful Structural Adjustment Plan*, Discussion Paper Series No 634, Centre For Economic Policy Research.

Breward, C. (1995), *The Culture of Fashion*, Manchester, Manchester University Press.

Brewer, J. and Porter, R. (1993), *Consumption and the World of Goods*, London, Routledge.

Bull, A., Pitt, M. and Szarka, J. (1993), *Entrepreneurial Textile Communities: A Comparative Study of Small Textile and Clothing Firms*, London, Chapman & Hall.

Butazzi, G. (1980), *1922–1943 Vent'Anni di Moda Italiana*, Florence, Centro Di.

Butazzi, G. et al. (1987), *Italian Fashion, Volume 1: The Origins of High Fashion and Knitwear*, and *Italian Fashion, Volume 2: From Anti-Fashion to Stylism*, Milan, Electa.

Butazzi, G. (1991), *Per Una Storia della Moda Pronta*, Florence, Edifir.

Carter, E. (1974), *With Tongue in Chic*, London, Michael Joseph.

Cawthorne, N. (1996), *The New Look: the Dior Revolution*, London, Hamlyn.

Celant, G. (ed.) (1994), *Italian Metamorphosis 1943–68*, New York, Guggenheim.

Celant, G., Settembrini, L. and Sischy, I. (1996), *Emilio Pucci: Looking at Fashion*, Biennale di Firenze.

Cento Bull, A. and Corner, P. (1993), *From Peasant To Entrepreneur: the Survival of the Family Economy in Italy*, Oxford, Berg.

Clark, M. (1984), *Modern Italy 1871–1982*, London, Longman.

Clough, S. B. (1964), *The Economic History of Modern Italy*, Columbia, Columbia University Press.

Conway, H. (ed.) (1987), *Design History: a Student's Handbook*, London, Allen and Unwin.

Crowley, D. (1992), *National Style and Nation State: Design in Poland from the Vernacular Revival to the International Style*, Manchester, Manchester University Press.

De la Haye, A. (ed.) (1997), *The Cutting Edge: 50 Years of British Fashion 1947–1997*, London, V&A.

De Petri, S. and Leventon, M. (1989), *New Look to Now: French Haute Couture 1947–1987*, New York, Rizzoli.

Duggan, C. and Wagstaff, C. (eds) (1995), *Italy in the Cold War: Politics, Culture and Society 1948–58*, Oxford, Berg.

Dulles, A. (1993), *The Marshall Plan*, Oxford, Berg.

Ellwood, D. (1985), *Italy 1943–1945*, Leicester, Leicester University Press.

Ellwood, D. (1992), *Rebuilding Western Europe: America and Postwar Reconstruction*, London, Longman.

Ellwood, D. and Kroes, R. (eds) (1994), *Hollywood in Europe: Experiences of a Cultural Hegemony*, Amsterdam, VU University Press.

Ewen, S. (1988), *All Consuming Images: the Politics of Style in Contemporary Culture*, New York, Basic Books.

Fontana, M. (1991), *Specchio a Tre Luci*, Turin, Nuova Eri.

Forgacs, D. (1990), *Culture in the Industrial Era 1880–1980: Cultural Industries, Politics and the Public*, Manchester, Manchester University Press.

Gastel, M. (1995), *50 Anni di Moda Italiana: Breve Storia del Prêt-à-Porter*, Milan, Domino/Avallardi.

Ginsborg, P. (1990), *A History of Contemporary Italy: Society and Politics 1943–88*, London, Penguin.

Giordani Aragno, B. (ed.) (1988), *Moda Italia: Creativita e Tecnologia alla Sistema della Moda Italiana*, Milan, Domus.

Gramsci, A. (1971), *Sections from the Prison Notebooks*, London, Lawrence and Wishart.

Gundle, S. (1996), 'The Americanisation of Daily Life: Television and Consumerism in Italy in the 1950s', *Italian Culture and Society*, 2.

Handlin, O. (1959), *Immigration as a Factor in American History*, New Jersey, Prentice Hall.

Harper, J. (1986), *America and the Reconstruction of Italy 1945–8*, Cambridge, Cambridge University Press.

Hobsbaum, E.J. (1990), *Nation and Nationalism since 1780: Programme, Myth, and Reality*, Cambridge, Cambridge University Press (second edition).

Hogan, M. (1987), *The Marshall Plan: America, Britain and the Reconstruction of Western Europe, 1947–1952*, Cambridge, Cambridge University Press.

Hughes, H. (1979), *The United States and Italy*, Cambridge, Mass./London, Harvard University Press (first published 1953).

Hutchinson, J. and Smith, A. (eds) (1994), *Nationalism*, Oxford, Oxford University Press.

Kennedy, S. (1991), *Pucci: a Renaissance in Fashion*, New York, Abbeville Press.

Kidwell, C. and Christman, M. (1974), *Suiting Everyone: the Democratisation of Clothing in America*, Washington D.C., Smithsonian Institute.

King, R. (1987), *Italy*, London, Harper & Row.

Koda, H., Martin, R. and Sinderbrand, L. (eds) (1987), *Three Women: Madeleine Vionnet, Claire McCardell and Rei Kawakubo*, New York, FIT.

Le Bourhis, K., Ricci, S. and Settimbrini, L. (1996), *Emilio Pucci: Looking at Fashion*, Florence, Skira.

Lee Levin, P. (1965), *The Wheels of Fashion*, New York, Doubleday.

Levitt, S. (1986), *Victorians Unbuttoned*, London, Allen and Unwin.

Liatra Ponti, L. (1990), *Gio Ponti: the Complete Work 1923–1978*, London, Thames and Hudson.

McCardell, C. (1956), *What Shall I Wear? The What, Where, When and How Much of Fashion*, New York.

Maeder, E. (1988), *Hollywood and History*, London, Thames and Hudson.

Maier, C. (ed.) (1978), *The Origins of the Cold War and Contemporary Europe*, New York, New Viewpoints.

Massoni, Luigi, (ed.) (1986), *Made in Italy*, Milan, Mondadori.

Meikle, J. (1979), *Twentieth Century Limited: Industrial Design in America, 1925–39*, Philadelphia, Temple.

Milward, A. (1984), *The Reconstruction of Western Europe 1945–51*, London, Methuen.

Nelli, H. (1983), *From Immigrants to Ethnics: the Italian-Americans*, Oxford, Oxford University Press.

Nystrom, P. (1928), *The Economics of Fashion*, New York, Ronald Press.

Radice, B. (1993), *Ettore Sottsass: a Critical Biography*, London, Thames and Hudson.

Rennolds Milbank, C. (1989), *New York Fashion: the Evolution of American Style*, New York, Abrams.

Ricci, S. (ed.) (1995), *Salvatore Ferragamo: the Art of the Shoe*, Milan, Mondadori.

Smart Martin, A. (1993), 'Makers, Buyers and Users – Consumerism as a Material Culture Framework', *Winterthur Portfolio*, Vol. 28, 2–4, Summer-Autumn.

Sparke, P. (1982), *Ettore Sottsass Jnr.*, London, Design Council.

Sparke, P. (1988), *Italian Design 1870 to the Present*, London, Thames and Hudson.

Steele, V. (1988), *Paris Fashion: a Cultural History*, New York, Oxford University Press.

Steele, V. (1991), *Women of Fashion: Twentieth Century Designers*, New York, Rizzoli.

Thompson, P. (1988), *The Voice of the Past: Oral History*, Oxford, Oxford University Press (first published 1978).

Tomlinson, A. (ed.) (1990), *Consumption, Identity and Style: Marketing, Meanings and the Packaging of Pleasure*, London, Routledge.

Vergani, G. (1992), *La Sala Bianca: the Birth of Italian Fashion*, Milan, Electa.

Walker, J. (1989), *Design History and the History of Design*, London, Pluto.

Wilson, E. (1985), *Adorned in Dreams: Fashion and Modernity*, London, Virago.

Wilson, E. and Taylor, L. (1989), *Through the Looking Glass: a History of Dress from 1860 to the Present*, London, BBC.

Woolf, S.J. (ed.) (1972), *The Rebirth of Italy 1943–50*, London, Longman.

Yohannan, K. (1998), *Claire McCardell: Redefining Modernism*, New York, Harry N. Abrams.

Zamagni, V. (1993), *The Economic History of Italy 1860–1990*, Oxford, Clarendon.

Index